My Journey from Shanghai to Las Vegas

An Autobiography

by Bert Reiner

TO LEN & LINDA!
TO OUR DEAR FRIENDS, &
DEAR NEIGHBOR &
CONTRIBUTOR/EDITOR

Bert

TO OUR DEAR LINDA!
TO OUR DEAR NEIGHBOR, FRIENDS &
CONTRIBUTOR/EDITOR

In Memory of my father (Papi) and mother (Omi), without whom my survival would not have been possible.

In Dedication to the love of my life Sandy, our children Helaine, Eric and Dana, their spouses, and their children. This is for you, to remember your heritage.

Table of Contents

Prologue

As early as 1919, Adolf Hitler, in the form of a letter, wrote about anti-Semitism. In this letter, he presented for the first time many of the obsessions about Jewish people - revolving around greed, Jews as a race, and Jews refusing to assimilate. Towards the end of this letter, Hitler equated Jews with being a "Racial Tuberculosis" and proposed his "Final Solution" by stating that the ultimate objective must be the irrevocable removal of the Jews. In this early writing, it was thought that he meant removal of Jews from Germany, but it later became clear that his true meaning was the removal of ALL Jews from the face of the earth. At the time, Hitler's words were just words, but, he repeated and propagated those words to the point that it compelled a nation to act and eventually became the darkest time in our history.

Recently, on October 27, 2018 we saw the slaughter of eleven Jews at the *Tree of Life Congregation* in Pittsburgh, PA, right here in the U.S.A. Today, we see anti-Semitism on the rise in Europe, on our universities, and all over this country. There must not be a repetition of *Kristallnacht--,* **never again*!*.

See my journey and history that followed that infamous night in 1938:

All About Me

Me: On May 30, 1937, I was born *Norbert (Bert) Leo Reiner* at 41 *Louisenalle Strasse* Dresden, Saxony, Germany. At my *brith*, I was named *Yeshiya Ben Meir Hacohen*. I was named 'Norbert' after my father's best friend *Norbert Strier*; although my mother had opposed that name because it was not traditional to be named after someone still living, but my father insisted. He also persuaded my parents to emigrate to Shanghai (which most probably saved our lives).

People born in 1937 (the Year of the Ox in the Chinese zodiac), are deemed to have the characteristics of endurance, diligence, caution, persistence and honesty. As a child, I was known to be precocious, technical (always wanted to become an engineer), and my love of young kids and animals.

Some of my favorite things and places were:

Foods: Lamb Shanks (as an infant I called it *'gute fleish'*); Weiner schnitzel; Peking duck; tiger prawns; Hungarian goulash (only my mother's recipe); crab; caviar (black or red); milk chocolate; fried rice (sub gum) and French fries (Nathan's), cervalat wurst (salami).

TV Shows: "Twilight Zone"; "Alf"; "Dallas"; "Falcon Crest"; "Law & Order"; "Six Million Dollar Man"; "Candid Camera"; "Mission Impossible" and "Colombo".

Sports: soccer; swimming (breast-stroke); hockey (field); boxing; golf (with *Ira Rosenmertz*); racquetball (with *Larry Karam*); ice-Skating and skiing.

Hobbies: photography; stamp collecting; HO trains; coin collecting; build/fly model planes; 3D pictures; growing bonsai, and genealogy.

9

Music: Strauss waltzes; piano instrumentals; "West Side Story"; "Madame Butterfly"; Carpenters; Liberace; Whitney Houston; "Phantom of the Opera"; "Les Miserable" and the Three Tenors.

Movies: "Robinson Crusoe"; James Bond 007 movies; "Star Wars"; "Bodyguard"; "Out of Towners"; "Gentlemen's Agreement"; "Paperclip"; "Dr. Zhivago"; "Big"; "Exodus"; "Jaws" and Alfred Hitchcock movies.

Books: "A Connecticut Yankee in King Arthur's Court" (Mark Twain); "Jungle Book" (Rudyard Kipling); "Treasure Island" (Robert L. Stevenson); "War and Peace" (Leon Tolstoy), "James Bond 007" (Ian Fleming); "The Other Side of Midnight" (Sidney Sheldon); "Gulliver's Travels" (Jonathan Swift); "Of Human Bondage" (Summerset Maugham); and "Sherlock Holmes" (Sir Arthur C. Doyle).

Events: Annual camping trips with Eric and Dana; Learning to ski at the A-Frame in Maine; Becoming a U.S. citizen (12-29-1955); Ice skating with Popi at Radio City (1-28-1957); Sandy and I getting married in Troy (6-25-1960); Omi's 100th birthday in Clifton (2-23-2005); Caryl & Marv's 50th anniversary in Las Vegas (10-9-2005); and Great Wildebeest Migration in Africa (6-25-2017).

Ancient Sites I've visited: Jerusalem; Caesarea [Israel]; Rome; Acropolis [Athens]; Pompeii; Ephesus [Turkey]; Great Wall of China; Forbidden City [Beijing]; Niagara Falls; Sedona and Grand Canyon.

Beautiful Women: Kim Novak (Vertigo); Halle Berry (Die Another Day); Gal Hadith (Wonder Woman); Grace Kelly (Rear Window); Catherine Zeta Jone (Oceans's Twelve); Ursula Andres (Dr. No); and Priyanka Chopra (Quantico).

Zoos: San Diego Animal Reserve; San Diego Zoo; Bronx Zoo; Beardsley Park; Shanghai (pandas); Memphis; London; Bush Gardens; Kenya (baby elephants); Ramat Gan (Israel).

Innovations: from Slide-rules to Calculators; from Radio to Big-screen TV; from Ovens to Microwaves; from Film cameras to iPhones; from 33rpm records to Digital; from Coin-op phones to Cell phones; from Mimeograph to Xerox printers; from Stick-shift transmission to Automatic; from Telex to Fax; and from Pong to Playstation.

Clubs: Boy Scouts; Rotary; Computer club; Genealogy club; and Holocaust survivors group.

Holocaust Films: "The Boy in Stripped Pajamas"; "Europa-Europa"; "Schindler's List"; "Judgment at Nuremburg"; "Diary of Anne Frank"; "The Pianist"; "Defiance"; "Sarah's Key" and "Once We Were Brothers".

Memorial Sites: Theresienstad CC [Prague]; Riga CC [Latvia]; Mathausen CC [Vienna]; 9-11 Memorial [NYC]; Yad Vashem [Israel]; Holocaust Memorial [Berlin]; Oklahoma City [OK]; Baha'i Temple [Haifa]; Dome-of-the-Rock [Jerusalem]; Wailing Wall, Chiang Kai-Shek [Taipei].

Hate: Things I dislike most: Filling up gas tank (I wait till it reads 'E'); seeing the dentist (even though I never have cavities); Sea cucumber (Chinese); Sufriet (lungs); Beaches (don't like the sand); Shopping; Wasting food (having seen so many people starving); Thin toilet paper; or Shaving (*don't have to do very often now that I'm retired*).

More about me later...

Papi and his Parents

Horace: On January 1, 1907, my father, *Horst (Horace) William Reiner* (affectionately known as 'Papi'). was born in the city of Dresden, Saxony, Germany At his *brith*, he was named *Meir Ben Moishe Hacohen*. He grew up in Dresden, graduating from the *Commercial Gymnasium,* (university). He worked at *M.Albersheim*, then later at his father's department store, *Kaufhaus Reiner*.

Horace was extremely bright. When he would apply for jobs after we came to the U.S., he was generally found to be over-qualified. Eventually, he received a position in the International department with Bache & Co. He then studied to be licensed broker. His grades were far superior to the others.

My parents met on a blind date at a masquerade ball, and were married on March 15, 1932 in Frankfurt, their first born was *Egon Manfred* (died August 12, 1935) due to complications at birth. I followed two years later.

12

STORY: When I was about ten, I remember, on a Sunday morning, my parents and I were eating breakfast, and my egg had two yokes. My father asked my mother to leave the room, and he then proceeded to tell me about 'the birds and the bees.'

My father was a wonderful man, he loved everyone, and everyone loved him. He and I were very extremely close, he was truly my best friend. We did everything together, taking walks, doing homework, and collecting stamps.

Unfortunately, my father died on March 27, 1957, at age 50 of *Lympho-Sarcoma Cancer*. He is buried at *Cedar Park Cemetery*, Paramus, NJ, near his father.

Maximilian: My paternal grandfather was *Maximilian Reiner* (born March 12, 1878 in Dresden, died February 5, 1949 in NYC). He was married to *Elsa Emma Rössler* (born on December 4, 1877 in Dresden, died in 1966). In 1940, shortly after the war started, Maximilian was sent to a hard-labor camp at *Sachsenhausen Concentration Camp* in Frankfurt, Germany, and then on November 1, 1944 he was sent on to *Theresienstadt Concentration Camp* in Prague, Czechoslovakia. The latter was known as a 'good' concentration camp, often being used by the Nazis for propaganda and allowing the Red Cross to show how well the inmates were being treated.

My grandfather survived the war, two concentration camps, and in 1948 managed to emigrate to the U.S. But unfortunately died of a heart-attack only six months before my parents and I arrived. He is buried (perpetual care) near his son, at *Cedar Park Cemetery*, Paramus, NJ.

Elsa: My grandmother *Elsa* was not Jewish (she was Lutheran) but converted to Judaism when she married my grandfather. However, when the war progressed, she renounced her Judaism in order to survive the war.

STORY: When we first moved into our home in Kew Garden Hills, my father wrote to his mother in Germany, describing our apartment that we had five closets. My grandmother queried why a family of three would have five *toilets* (in German a '*closet*' means toilet).

STORY: After we arrived in the U.S., periodically my father sent 'CARE' packages to his mother, living in East Germany. He would write on the outside of the package '*gift*' which was frequently confiscated (in German '*gift*' means poison).

As the Communist regime would not allow my grandmother to come to visit her son in the U.S.; she remained in Dresden, Germany; together with my aunt *Kate* and uncle *Guenther Mickwausch*. In 1960, my father did finally manage to visit them in East Germany. She continued to live there under Communist rule (as she had no choice), until she died in 1966, at age 89.

QUOTE: **"Be ever ready to learn, be tolerant, be broad minded".** *Horace Reiner*

QUOTE: **"Achievement is the only enduring satisfaction in life".** *Horace Reiner*.

Omi and her Parents

Omi: On February 23, 1905, my mother *Gertrude (Trudy) Kahn* (affectionately known as 'Omi'), was born in Schotten, Frankfurt, Germany, named *Gutrud Bat Moshe Hacohen*. She had a long and healthy life, living to 2007 (she died peacefully on her 102nd birthday), at *Daughters of Miriam* in Clifton, NJ.

Ida: My grandmother *Ida Salberg,* died giving birth to *Lieselotte;* so my mother, at age 12, became the surrogate 'mother' to her five siblings. After *Kristallnacht*, my aunt *Hertha* and uncle *Max* emigrated to the U.S. My aunt *Ilse* at age 17 was a staunch Zionist, fled to Palestine. But *Lotte* (my mother's youngest sister) stayed behind.

Salli: Sometime during 1943- *Salli Kahn,* my mother's father, together with his youngest daughter Lotte, were both exterminated in the *Litzmannstadt Concentration Camp*, in Lodz, Poland. (We found this out during our visit to *Yad Vashem*).

15

A Little History

[1] **Jan 30, 1933** – ADOLF HITLER IS APPOINTED CHANCELLOR.

Sep, 1933- JEWS ARE NO LONGER ALLOWED TO OWN LAND.

Aug, 1934 - PRESIDENT VON HINDENBURG DIES AND HITLER BECOMES FÜHRER. HE RECEIVES A **90 %** YES VOTE FROM GERMAN VOTERS .

Sept, 1935 – *'NUREMBERG RACE LAWS'* AGAINST JEWS: DEFINED THAT A "NON-ARYAN IS ANY JEW BORN FROM EITHER NON-ARYAN PARENTS OR GRANDPARENTS; ANY INTER-MARRIAGE IS PUNISHABLE BY PRISON".

Jan, 1937- JEWS IN GERMANY ARE BANNED FROM PRACTICING MANY PROFESSIONS I.E. TEACHERS, ACCOUNTANTS, DOCTORS OR LAWYERS.

Dec, 1937- JAPAN INVADES SHANGHAI, THEN NANKING, KILLING OVER **600,000** CHINESE (THE RAPE OF NANJING).

March, 1938 - NAZI TROOPS ENTER AUSTRIA, HITLER ANNOUNCES THE *"ANSCHLUSS"* (ANNEXATION), MORE *"LEBENSRAU*M" (LIVING SPACE)

July, 1938 - AT EVIAN, FRANCE, THE LEAGUE OF NATIONS HOLDS A CONFERENCE WITH DELEGATES FROM **32** COUNTRIES TO CONSIDER HELPING JEWS FLEE HITLER. NO COUNTRY WOULD ACCEPT THEM, AND THE UNITED STATES CONTINUES TO LIMIT IT'S IMMIGRATION TO IT'S 'QUOTA' SYSTEM. THOSE JEWS WHO WAITED PATIENTLY FOR BETTER TIMES, ARE FINALLY CONVINCED TO FLEE; BUT IS IT TOO LATE?

Aug, 1938 - NAZIS REQUIRE JEWISH WOMEN TO ADD <u>SARAH</u>, AND MEN TO ADD <u>ISRAEL</u> TO THEIR NAMES IN THEIR PASSPORTS FOR THOSE THAT DID NOT HAVE ' TYPICALLY JEWISH' NAMES, STAMPED WITH A RED "J".

Nov 9, 1938 –ERNST VON RATH, SECRETARY TO THE GERMAN EMBASSY IN PARIS, IS SHOT BY THE **17** YEAR OLD SON OF ONE OF THE DEPORTED POLISH JEWS. THIS PRECIPITATED *'KRISTALLNACHT'* (NIGHT OF BROKEN GLASS). NAZIS THEN FINE THE JEWS ONE BILLION MARKS FOR DAMAGES RELATED TO THAT NIGHT.

16

Part 1

My Shanghai Memoirs
(1939 - 1949)

Our Departure

KRISTALLNACHT (NIGHT OF BROKEN GLASS) On November 9, 1938, a 17 year old Jewish youth in Paris shot the Secretary of the German Embassy. In response to this action, and as an excuse to further anti-Semitism, the Nazis unleashed an orgy of hatred and destruction throughout Germany. The toll was staggering, with scores of synagogues destroyed, over 7,000 Jewish businesses trashed, over 30,000 Jews arrested, and upwards of 100 killed. My father decided it was time to leave his homeland. His best friend *Norbert Strier* (after whom I was named), suggested we find refuge in either Kobe, Japan or Shanghai, China. As Asians did not have the same tradition of anti-Semitism, we believed they respected and admired the Jewish people. At the time, emigrating to Shanghai seemed crazy, but it was a decision that ultimately saved our lives. My father did not, and could not, believe what would happen, did in fact, happen.

[2] **"Why Shanghai? That question has been asked by many throughout the years about the flight of Jews from Nazi Europe to Shanghai. This episode of World War II remains a quirk of history, and few people knew that this escape route existed. The answer to the question is simple, painfully so: The world, including the United States and England, while expressing sympathy, closed its doors to Jews seeking refuge from the Nazis and the Holocaust."**

17

In the days after *Kristallnacht*, queues are formed at immigration offices at dawn. Whole days were spent getting clearances from the police, paying fees to depart, and then turning over all their remaining money to the Nazis. There were countless visits to consular offices to obtain transit visas but very few countries (including the United States), were willing to take any Jews. China, however, did not require entry-visas or passports. The only thing required to go to China was money to purchase transport. My parents told me later it was very difficult for them to depart their home and country of birth: my mother left her father and little sister (both were later exterminated); my father left both his parents, sister and business behind. They had no interest in journeying halfway across the globe. Thinking everything would blow over, their parents refused to go. But why Shanghai? As far as we knew, it was the only port in the world (besides the Dominican Republic) willing to accept Jews exiled from Germany.

My parents purchased a forty-foot container called a '*Lift*' in which we packed all our furniture and belongings. Many of these items were later sold or bartered for our basic survival in Shanghai. My mother gave the packer all her jewelry, in the hopes that he would smuggle them with the furniture, but she did not know if he would hide it, keep it, or turn us over to the Nazis. Packers were under strict Nazi scrutiny, and if he had been caught, his actions would probably have been punishable by death. Several years after our arrival in Shanghai, at a dinner party, the lights went out due to an electrical short. We found that all the jewelry had been hidden inside the arms of our crystal chandelier. Here was a 'good' German who risked his life to help us. The Nazis, meanwhile, allowed us to leave, but with only *10marks* per person (equivalent to only U.S. $2.50).

18

On March 6th 1939 the Reiners departed Germany via the *SS Potsdam,* a *Nord Deutscher Lloyd* luxury liner, traveling from Bremenhaven, Germany, to Genoa Italy, around the Suez Canal, to Kobe Japan, Hong Kong, and then finally to Shanghai, China. Although traveling in 1st class, we were still faced with extreme prejudice; we were given the following notice:

> *"We request that the non-Aryan German passengers not use the Swimming Pool or Gymnasium between the hours of 10:00am and 3:00pm...*
> *The Captain".*

19

This is what my father wrote in the diary he prepared for my Bar Mitzvah:

[3] **"You were growing normally as a child should grow, but not as fast as these photos make you believe, and in between there were times, when we were worried-just in the way as all the parents were doing all over the world. The photos are the best proof that you were a healthy child. Actually, our worries concentrated on our future as life became unbearable in Germany during 1938 and we contemplated our emigration. We left Germany in March 1939 for China and the following pictures were taken on the s/s Potsdam which brought us to Shanghai".**

Aboard ship we met *Analiese & Fritz Wolf*, and *Ilse & Erwin DeJong*, who become our life-long friends.

On March 28th, after our long journey, we finally arrived in Shanghai. We now are *Shanghailanders*. Upon arrival, we were immunized for smallpox, then greeted by *Laura Margolis* of the *Joint Distribution Committee* (JDC)

20

and led to the *Embankment Building* to secure our housing. We were given the following instructions written in German and English:

1. Orders given are to be followed without fail.
2. Political discussions are strictly forbidden.
3. It is forbidden to take photos, or carrying cameras.
4. Conspicuous conduct and loud conversation on the streets are forbidden.
5. It is forbidden to enter nightclubs, and to participate in gambling of any kind.
6. It is compulsory for those who receive monetary assistance to participate in English language courses
7. Be warned of pickpockets.

There were three separate Jewish communities in Shanghai: the first were the Sephardic Jews, who came from Iraq at the turn of the century. The *David Sassoon* family (known as the 'Rothschilds of the East') came to Shanghai in 1844 to commence trade with China, and were soon followed by the *Sassoon, Hardoon* and *Kadoorie* families. With extreme foresight, they bought land cheaply; established banking and commerce; traded in textiles, silk and opium; and quickly prospered. They built much of the buildings on the *Bund*, including the magnificent *Cathay Hotel, Sassoon House*, the *Bank of China*, the *Yokohama Bank*, the *Jardine Matheson & Co.*, and the *Customs House* (with the large clock-tower).

The second wave of immigration to Shanghai were the *Ashkenazi* 'white' Russian Jews who fled the Bolshevik Pogroms and Revolution of 1917.

The third wave were the German, Polish, Austrian, Lithuanian and other East-European Jews who, like us, escaped Hitler's holocaust. In contrast to the first two phases, the Ashkenazi refugees were often downtrodden, penniless, and viewed Shanghai as a temporary stop. Some well known immigrants living there were *Michael Blumenthal* (later became U.S. Secretary of Treasury), *Peter Max* (famous U.S. pop-artist), and *Herbert Zernik* (comedian).

Many American movies were being shown. In a copy of the *Shanghai Jewish Chronicle* (dated January 12, 1942), I noted the following movies were playing: "Aloma of the South Seas", with Dorothy Lamour; "The Bride came to C.O.D." with James Cagney; "The Man with Nine Lives" with Boris Karloff; and "Boom Town" with Clark Gable.

Chiune Sempo Sugihara was the Japanese Consul General in Kovno, Lithuania, who had furnished 4,163 visas to his constituents for travel to Kobe, Japan. *Ho Feng Shan* was the Chinese Consul in Vienna had supplied 2,000 visas.

At that time, Shanghai had the world's largest population and the 5th greatest harbor in the world. *Jacob Sassoon* started the Sephardic synagogue *Ohel Rachel*; and *Silas Hardoon* started the Ashkenazi *Beth Aharon* synagogue. There were forty-six distinct groups of expatriates in Shanghai. At the top were the British who comprised 40% of the foreigners. They brought Sikhs to serve as policemen, guards, and doormen. (easily recognized wearing turbans).

   Sir Horace Kadoorie started the Shanghai Jewish Youth Association School (commonly known as the SJYA or simply the Kadoorie school); which I attended (*I'm seated in the 4th from left, in the 2nd row*). Seen also is *Evelyn Wolpert* (*she's seated in the 2nd from right, in the 1st row*) who now lives in Las Vegas. During those years, there were six synagogues and four Jewish cemeteries. Arriving in Shanghai, we were faced with abysmal sanitation and rampant diseases. Most refugees arrived with most, if not all, their belongings either confiscated or forcibly sold. What little money they had left, was spent on their journey to Shanghai. Except for the Germans, most of the refugee community spoke Yiddish, as did the Russians. We were very grateful for the sincere help we got from the wealthy and established Baghdadi Jews.

   [4] "The realization that it is by them that the Jewish community would be judged and the opinion of other races towards the Jews in general would be formed, made it clearly our duty to give our Jewish youth a fair start in life, and try to teach them the responsibilities of being a Jew". *Horace Kadoorie*

   Shortly after our arrival, my father was stricken with *Spinal-Meningitis*; was put in quarantine, and not expected to live. My mother found herself in a foreign country, with a

23

husband not expected to survive, with no knowledge of the language, no jewelry to pawn, and no money. She really had to struggle, with a dying husband (because of fear of contagion, the hospital even denied her visitations to see him), and a young toddler (me) to care for. Their best friend *Norbert Strier* was supposed to have held their money, but he said that he lost it due to some bad investments. (We later found out that he had swindled it all). We never spoke with him again.

My father miraculously survived and we were a whole family again. Firstly we moved into an apartment on 255 Route Cohen in the more prestigious *French Concession*. Living here was not too bad.

We did appreciate having left Germany when we did, after all, it did save our lives. The exodus from Europe to Shanghai was expanding and Shanghai was getting extremely crowded. The refugees came via ships from Germany, Italy, England, and even through Vladivostok via the Trans-Siberian Railway. It was an enormous problem for the comparatively small Jewish community to cope with the thousands of fleeing brethren coming to this city.

My parents talked about Shanghai as being the *"Paris of the Orient."* For us, it meant a place of welcome, freedom, and opportunity, but these promises would soon fall short. Just as Hitler wanted to master all of Europe, Japan wanted to take over all of Asia, and even America. Fortunately for us, the Japanese didn't discriminate against Jews, all Europeans were equally known as *'Gwailo'* (white devils).

Fuel was at a premium. Food was scarce, my mother cooked rice or beans on a charcoal stove, then placed the pot into my bed to keep both the food and my bed warm. People got around in *rickshaws* or, the more modern 3-wheeled *'pedicabs'*.

Dec, 1938- THE UNITED KINGDOM RESCUED NEARLY 10,000 CHILDREN BETWEEN THE AGES OF 2-17 FROM GERMANY, AUSTRIA, AND CZECHOSLOVAKIA AND SENT THEM TO PRIVATE FAMILIES IN ENGLAND.

May, 1939- THE *SS ST. LOUIS*, A SHIP CROWDED WITH 930 JEWISH REFUGEES, IS TURNED AWAY BY BOTH CUBA AND THE UNITED STATES. THE 1924 IMMIGRATION ACT SET FIRM LIMITS TO THE NUMBER OF IMMIGRANTS WHO COULD ENTER THE U.S. NO OTHER COUNTRY ALLOWED THE SHIP TO PORT, SO IT RETURNED TO EUROPE, WHERE OVER HALF WERE LATER EXTERMINATED.

April, 1940 - NAZIS INVADE DENMARK AND NORWAY, FOLLOWED BY FRANCE, BELGIUM, HOLLAND & LUXEMBOURG. THE *TRIPARTITE PACT* (KNOWN AS THE AXIS FORCES) SIGNED BY GERMANY, ITALY & JAPAN.

On April 17, 1941, my father, together with his partners *Fritz Wolf* (whom we had met aboard ship), and *Max Fleischman* (a wealthy Russian Jew living in Harbin, Manchuria) merged to form an import-export business named *Fleischmann Impex Company*. But the war put a freeze on any international trade, so as a result, the company lay dormant as a result. This is what my father wrote in my diary:

[3] "The year 1941 brought us much excitement as the clouds of war drew nearer and nearer to the Pacific. Of course, you did not know anything about this. You went to school and enjoyed life, your friends and parties. But your parents worried much, especially for your grandfather's (Momi's and Popi's father) who wanted to leave Germany but were unable to do so, as the war in Europe had started.

And then…. Suddenly we were again in the midst of war as the Japanese had their sneak attack on Pearl Harbor. Hectic days followed, proclamations were posted everywhere, many things were prohibited, even listening to any short-wave radios.

Sometime later we had to surrender to the Japanese authorities our beautiful radio which we had brought from Germany. Thousands of Jewish refugees suffered most as they were cut off the main source of their financing. Prices went sky high, especially for food. Another Chinese currency was created by the Japanese and introduced by force – it was called Central Reserve Bank notes, or CRB".

Economic help was obtained primarily from the Sephardic Jews already living in Shanghai, and from the *Jewish Joint Committee* (JJC) of New York. Food was distributed as needed through the '*Kitchen Fund*'. A hospital was set up with refugee doctors distributing medicines (when available) gratis to all Jews. In the *Heimes* (homes), there were shared toilets, no hot water, no lights, and no privacy.

My father, not being able to work in his field, shifted his focus to helping the refugees secure money and food, upon which they depended for their sustenance.

I attended the *Wonderland Kindergarten,* oblivious to what was happening around me. Most of the refugees lived in dismal and cramped apartments, some shared with several hundreds per room. These conditions were atrocious. Hygiene was a perpetual problem. Eventually, the exodus out of Europe had slowed. There were now almost 18,000 German, Austrian, Polish and Lithuanian Jewish refugees; plus another 5,000 Russians; and the few (wealthy) Iraqi Jews who helped the less fortunate. My family employed an *amah* (servant), who also served as my nanny.

June, 1941- NAZIS INVADE SOVIET UNION- NAMED 'OPERATION BARBAROSA'.

July, 1941 – HEINRICH HIMMLER SUMMONS THE AUSCHWITZ COMMANDER: "*THE FÜHRER HAS ORDERED THE FINAL SOLUTION OF THE JEWISH QUESTION*". THE FIRST USE OF 'ZYKLON-B' GAS IS TESTED AT AUSCHWITZ. ALSO, **3,800** JEWS ARE KILLED DURING A PROGRAM BY LITHUANIANS IN KOVNO.

Sep, 1941- THE HUNGARIAN ARMY ROUNDS UP **18,000** JEWS AT KAMENETS. THE SS MURDER **33,771** JEWS AT *BABI YAR* NEAR KIEV; AND ANOTHER **35,000** JEWS FROM ODESSA ARE SHOT.

Nov, 1941 - *THERESIENSTADT* CONCENTRATION CAMP IS ESTABLISHED IN CZECHOSLOVAKIA, TO BE USED AS A 'MODEL' GHETTO FOR PROPAGANDA PURPOSES, AND FOR INSPECTIONS BY THE RED CROSS.

Dec, 1941- ALL GERMAN JEWS OVER 10 YEARS OLD, ARE ORDERED TO WEAR A YELLOW '*STAR-OF-DAVID*' ARM-BANDS.

Dec 7, 1941- SHORTLY AFTER THE U.S. HAD MOVED THEIR PACIFIC FLEET TO HAWAII, THE JAPANESE IMPERIAL AIR FORCE MAKES A SURPRISE ATTACK ON THE NAVAL BASE AT PEARL HARBOR, WITH 6 AIRCRAFT-CARRIERS AND 183 FIGHTER PLANES, KILLING 2,403.

Dec 8, 1941- THE UNITED STATES DECLARES WAR ON JAPAN AND ENTERS THE WORLD WAR.

Dec 11, 1941- GERMANY DECLARES WAR ON THE UNITED STATES.

Dec, 1941- JAPAN INVADES MALAYA [MALAYSIA] AND THEN FOLLOWED BY BURMA [MYANMAR].

Feb, 1942- JAPAN INVADES SINGAPORE.

The Germans create *"Lebensborn"*, this was an SS initiated organization consisting of only 'pure' Aryans. To join, one must be at least 6' tall, blonde, with blue eyes, and at least 6th generation Aryan.

Pearl Harbor

On Dec 8, 1941 (Dec 7 in the U.S.), Japan attacked the United States naval base at *Pearl Harbor*. (Hawaii was then a U.S. Territory). The next day, the United States and Britain declared war on Japan, and WW II was in full bloom on all continents. Churchill was happy with the United States' entry into the war, because England finally had an ally to help in their defense against Hitler. We in China were extremely worried of what was to happen next, we sincerely hoped that the U.S. would soon end the war.

In Shanghai, this event of course dramatically changed our lives; communication with the outside world stopped; although we were able to write brief 25-word messages on flimsy paper transmitted through the International Red Cross, (to which we seldom received a reply). Travel around Shanghai became restricted food and medicine became scarce.

Meanwhile, my paternal grandfather, *Maximilian,* was sent to hard-labor at *Sachsenhausen* concentration camp, then went on to the *Theresienstad* concentration camp. Incredibly he survived the war, and was able to emigrate to the U.S.

29

Gestapo Colonel *Josef Meisinger,* the infamous *'Butcher of Warsaw'*, was sent to Shanghai to meet the Japanese high command to discuss the 'Jewish Solution.' His goal was to pressure the Japanese into liquidating the Hongkew Ghetto and all of it's Jewish inhabitants. Fortunately, the Japanese refused to consider any plans to exterminate any of the Jews.

It's important to note why the Japanese treated the Jewish community so well (as opposed to Nazi Germany): [5] Japan looked to Jews as *Fugu* (a very delicious, but also poisonous blow-fish). In the 1930s the most influential Japanese military officers, bankers, industrialists and politicians debated the most effective methods to fulfill their desired destiny of a world empire. Rather than via military expansion, why not conscript the best of the world's tradesmen and manufacturers, people who knew how to make quality goods, raise financing, and develop markets. As a policy, the Japanese decided that they needed the Jews. Thus was born *'The Fugu Plan'* designed to take in Europe's Jewry from the Nazi's and bring them to Manchuria, though this plan was never initiated.

Jan, 1942 – THE *WANNSEE* CONFERENCE IS HELD TO COORDINATE THE 'FINAL SOLUTION' THE SS REPORT THAT **229,000** JEWS HAD ALREADY BEEN EXTERMINATED TO DATE.

April, 1942- JEWS BANNED FROM USING ANY PUBLIC TRANSPORTATION.

June, 1942–THE SWISS REPRESENTATIVES OF THE *WORLD JEWISH CONGRESS* RECEIVE INFO THAT THE NAZIS PLAN TO EXTERMINATE ALL THE JEWS IN EUROPE; THIS IS RELAYED TO LONDON AND WASHINGTON, BUT NOTHING IS DONE!

July, 1942- HILTER ISSUES *'VERNICHTUNG DURCH ARBEIT'* (EXTERMINATION THROUGH LABOR).

July, 1942 - TREBLINKA EXTERMINATION CAMP IS OPENED IN POLAND, THE CAMP'S BUILDINGS CONTAIN 10 GAS CHAMBERS, EACH HOLDING 200 PERSONS; IT TAKES ONLY 60 MINUTES TO EXTERMINATE 2,000 PERSONS; THE BODIES ARE THEN BURNED IN OPEN PITS. JEWS AT AUSCHWITZ HAVE THEIR BANKNOTES, FOREIGN CURRENCY, GOLD AND JEWELS SENT TO SS HEADQUARTERS; WATCHES, CLOCKS AND PENS ARE DISTRIBUTED TO THE TROOPS; CLOTHING IS DISTRIBUTED TO NEEDY GERMAN FAMILIES.

Mar, 1943 - AMERICAN JEWS HOLD A MASS RALLY AT MADISON SQUARE GARDEN TO PRESSURE THE U.S. GOVERNMENT TO HELP THE JEWS OF EUROPE, BUT THEY ARE IGNORED.

April, 1943 – THE JEWISH RESISTANCE ATTACK THE SS WAFFEN IN THE WARSAW GHETTO; (THIS WAS THE FIRST OPEN REBELLION AGAINST THE GERMANS), BUT THAT WAS SOON SQUELCHED, WITH THOUSANDS OF JEWS SENT TO AUSCHWITZ AND EXTERMINATED.

May, 1943- NAZIS DECLARE BERLIN TO BE JUDENFREI (FREE OF JEWS).

Jan, 1944 - IN RESPONSE TO POLITICAL PRESSURE TO HELP JEWS UNDER NAZI CONTROL, ROOSEVELT ISSUES THE CONDEMNATION OF GERMAN AND JAPANESE AS "CRIMES AGAINST HUMANITY" CREATING THE WAR REFUGEE BOARD, BUT NOTHING GOT ACCOMPLISHED!

July, 1944 - SWEDISH DIPLOMAT RAOUL WALLENBERG FROM BUDAPEST, PROCEEDED TO SAVE 33,000 JEWS. FAILED ATTEMPT TO ASSASSINATE HITLER.

Aug, 1944 - ANNE FRANK AND HER FAMILY ARE ARRESTED BY GESTAPO IN AMSTERDAM, AND SENT TO AUSCHWITZ. ANNE IS LATER SENT TO BERGEN-BELSEN WHERE SHE DIES OF TYPHUS. WHILE IN HIDING; SHE HAD AUTHORED THE BOOK "DIARY OF ANNE FRANK". OSKAR SCHINDLER SAVES 1,200 JEWS BY MOVING THEM FROM A LABOR CAMP TO BRUNNLITZ; (THIS BECAME THE MOVIE "SCHINDLER'S LIST").

The Shanghai Proclamation

Soon, the Japanese brought even more dramatic hardships to the refugees. On Feb 18, 1943 the Japanese issued the *"Shanghai Proclamation"* to all Jewish 'stateless' refugees that immigrated into Shanghai after 1937. We were to move into a 'designated area' in the *Hongkew Ghetto*. This was the poorest part of Shanghai, only one-square mile with over 100,000 Chinese already living in squalor. We were fortunate, however, to move into 673 Dalney Road, a single-family villa (which we gladly shared with three other families), owned by my father's partner Max Fleischmann. There, we lived in relative luxury in comparison to other refugees, where hundreds were living in a *Heime* (home).

There's a lot that I have forgotten, but I remember being constantly hungry. I remember the poverty. I remember the nightmares. I remember walking to school past the bodies of people who had died of starvation or disease. I remember beggars asking me for money. I remember the heat. I remember the tapeworms in my stool.

CARD OF INDENTIFICATION

No. 2812

Photo with Signature of Bearer

ISSUED BY

INTERNATIONAL COMMITTEE

FOR GRANTING RELIEF TO

EUROPEAN REFUGEES

The Ghetto Walls were surrounded by barbed wire and guards with bayonets. Those wanting to travel outside were required to obtain a pass from *Kanoh Ghoya,* a cruel and irrational Japanese man, who named himself the *'King of the Jews.'* The refugees called him *'The Monkey.'* He was extremely short (about four feet tall) and did not take kindly to tall men, often slapping and humiliating them (my father was relatively short). He was bitter and sadistic, reveling in his position of power over the struggling refugees who were forced to beg for a temporary pass. The 'pass' was a round blue and white badge inscribed with the Chinese character for *'pass'*; valid for one to three months for travel outside the Ghetto walls.

For those of us who had been adjusting to living in the *French Settlement*, we found this new life in the Ghetto to be a terrible blow. Morale amongst the Jews have now sunk to their lowest level. Most refugees remained unemployed or survived through peddling of the belongings they brought from Europe. Professionals struggled and found no market for their skills. A few started driving taxis, delivering eggs, or working in a bakery or restaurant. My father, however, didn't do any of that; instead, he helped the other refugees as best he could.

For me, life went on; I celebrated my friend's fourth birthday party, (*I'm 4th from left, wasn't I cute?*). I attended the *Kadoorie* School, which had a beautiful Sephardic synagogue attached. Yet, the cultural life within the Ghetto was far more vibrant than one would expect. Many of these refugees had experienced the intellectual and artistic life of Europe and sought to recreate it here in Hongkew. Musicians performed in lively nightclubs and cafes and the *Shanghai Symphony Orchestra* was soon established. Besides them, there were also cantors, composers, artists, actors, and writers. Both German and English newspapers were published by the refugee community.

To maintain our health, we would always boil water, delivered to us by a *coolie* in wooden vats, before drinking, and <u>never</u> eating any raw vegetables. Growing up, I only drank '*Klim*' (milk spelled backwards). Despite these precautions, my family was stricken with *Dysentery*, *Jaundice*, *Typhoid Fever* (my mother became a carrier and later infected Helaine), *Diphtheria*, *Scarlet Fever*, *Typhus* (my father), *Malaria* (my mother), *Hoof-and-Mouth disease* (me, for which I was given gentian-violet for my mouth), and *Rabies* (I was bitten by a rabid dog, I got several shots in my stomach). Malnutrition and disease were so rampart that about 1,700 refugees had died in the Hongkew Ghetto.

For our protection, the men in the Jewish community formed their own police organization called the *Pao Chia*. All male refugees between the ages of 20-45 were required to volunteer for duty. My father served every two weeks, for 3 hours at a time, usually at night. They wore arm-bands, carried wooden sticks, and patrolled the Ghetto, enforcing the curfew and protecting the refugees.

The Jews and Chinese found a common bond that connected two ancient peoples together. But, the Chinese had suffered by the hands of the Japanese, more than did the Jews. Whole villages and cities were reduced to ash and rubble, families murdered, liberty removed; yet, in spite of their own plight, they showed immeasurable kindness and generosity towards the Jewish refugees, including my family.

Sometime during 1943, *Sally Kahn* (my mother's father) and *Lotte Kahn* (my mother's youngest sister), both having remained in Germany, were exterminated in the *Litzmannstadt Concentration* Camp, in Lodz, Poland. (This information was later found during our visit to *Yad Vashem*).

Holidays, Seders, Weddings and Bar Mitzvahs continued to nourish our spiritual needs. Rabbi *Georg Kantorowski* was our Ashkenazi rabbi who served the refugees well, and our cantor was *Heinz Wartenberger*. A German synagogue was started in the '*Jüdische Gemeinde*' (Jewish Community). As space in the synagogue in *Hongkew* was limited during the High Holidays, the services were conducted at the *Eastern Movie* Theater. Hebrew language and scriptures were taught in the *Kadoorie* School by *Lucie Hartwich,* our head-master. The school was built by *Horace Kadoorie*, a very philanthropic Jew from Iraq, conveniently located in the heart of the Jewish Ghetto where almost 600 students attended.

STORY: When I was young, the Jewish holidays maintained our sanity especially during Purim. There was an intense feeling when we stamped our feet and made noise to obliterate the name of *Haman*, (whom we associated with *Hitler*). When I was about 5 years old, I sat next to a hi-ranking Japanese Officer at a school function, who tried to befriend me by jokingly offering me a cigarette. To which I responded *"you dirty Jap"*; this could have led to our immediate execution, but he merely laughed.

Food was a severe scarcity, we generally ate from an assortment of different colored beans: purple, brown, black, yellow or white; we rarely ate meat. The JDC published in

36

The Shanghai Jewish Chronicle the following proclamation, to help the less fortunate immigrants:

1. [6] **Every family which does their own cooking, shall give daily at least (1) meal to a needy person.**
2. **Families which do not do their own cooking, shall pay a sum of $30 monthly instead.**
3. **Restaurants, coffee houses, and bars shall charge a 10% surtax on all bills.**
4. **Provision stores shall collect a 5% surtax on all goods sold.**

My family used one bathroom (we used newspaper instead of toilet paper); which we shared with my father's partner and his wife. It was a lot better than those other families living in the communal *Heime*.

STORY: To keep the drains free, to avoid flooding into the apartment; during one of the frequent Typhoons, my father leaned me out through a window. He held my feet, while I was upside-down, unclogging the drain in our 5th floor balcony, **WOW, that was scary**.

37

To bathe, we purchased hot water from a *coolie,* who carried two wooden buckets on a bamboo pole. He would empty the water into our bathtub and then my parents and I would successively take our baths in this precious hot water. We had a WC (wash-closet) that illegally emptied into the sewer, for which we had to pay a monthly *'kamsha'* (bribe). However, most other refugees relieved themselves in buckets which were emptied each morning into a *honey wagon* pulled by a *coolie* calling *"moo-dong."* The odor was quite revolting. Frequently, my mother picked lice out of my hair. Twice each year I was infected with tape-worms. I remember the heat, the diseases, and beggars chewing bark off trees. I remember seeing dead babies wrapped in straw lying along the street, abandoned because their parents could not afford a burial. I remember the Typhoons, violent downpours that lasted for days and days, with water up to my waist.

Because of the war, all metal had become very scarce: toothpaste tubes were saved for the zinc, tin-cans were used to build stove pipes, and one day it was announced that all bronze statues throughout Shanghai would be melted and used for munitions. The next day, the two lions in front of the *Hong Kong Shanghai Bank* (each weighing several tons) mysteriously disappeared. They were carried away by *coolies* and shipped to Hong Kong precariously on tiny *junks.*

38

The Shanghai experience was becoming very difficult. My parents had a hard time coping with survival in this strange and harsh environment. Conditions in the Ghetto became bleak and the future uncertain. My mother had an abortion, as she did not want to bring up any more children under these conditions. My parent's friends all had only one child, or none.

Some resourceful Chinese peddlers learned to speak some German; it was not unusual to hear a Chinese cobbler yelling "*Schuhmacher*" (shoemaker), or another who could fix broken plates "*Porzellan kaputte ganz machen*" (we can fix your porcelain).

To help the less fortunate Jewish refugees, a *Kitchen-Fund* was established to help feed and shelter them at the *Heime*, where my mother cooked daily, whilst my father was raising funds and sought food for them.

One day, while playing in our backyard, I noticed a warehouse fire erupting across the street. The Japanese immediately evacuated all the homes in the area. We too had to depart, leaving my father trapped while he removed the laundry from the roof which he feared might catch fire. It took three days to put out the fire. As we lived just across the street, dozens of Japanese soldiers were billeted in our house; it took that many days before my family was finally reunited again.

Growing up we did not have any pet dogs (having such an animal would not have lasted long; if it escaped, it surely would have been caught and slaughtered for food by some poor Chinese family). The only friend of ours that did have a dog (wire fox terrier) was the *Silverstein's*.

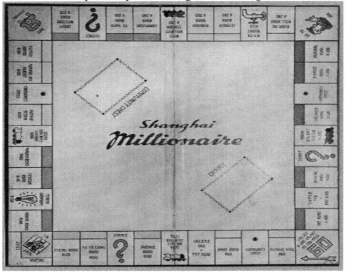

Playing with marbles was one of our favorite pastimes. Also popular was the board game '*Shanghai Millionaire*' (knock-off of Monopoly). The children of the Ghetto also invented their own games. One such game consisted of folding cigarette packs to about a 2" square. A ring was formed with chalk, and each player held his pack between his thumb and index finger and tried to knock out their opponent's pack.

During the last year of the war I remember hiding under our dining-room table, with a steel pot on my head, whenever the sirens sounded to announce the American bombs falling on Shanghai. The loud explosions still haunts me today; I jump awake upon hearing any sudden loud sounds. During these bombing raids, many of the Jews sought refuge in the courtyard of the *Hongkew* prison, which was supposedly protected against bombings by the *Geneva Conference*.

Jan, 1945- SOVIET TROOPS LIBERATE AUSCHWITZ, 1.5 MILLION JEWS WERE EXTERMINATED HERE.

Feb 4, 1945 – *YALTA CONFERENCE* HELD WITH ROOSEVELT, CHURCHILL AND STALIN. MARINES RAISE THE U.S. FLAG ON *IWO JIMA*.

Feb, 1945- THE U.S. BOMB DRESDEN SEVERELY INTO RUBBLE.

Apr 12, 1945- FRANKLIN D. ROOSEVELT DIES, TRUMAN TAKES OVER.

Apr 30, 1945 - HITLER COMMITS SUICIDE IN HIS BERLIN BUNKER.

Apr, 1945- THE BRITISH TROOPS LIBERATE *BERGEN-BELSON* CAMP.

May 8, 1945 – GERMANY UNCONDITIONAL SURRENDER; IT'S *VE DAY*. 6 MILLION JEWS WERE EXTERMINATED, 1/3 OF WORLD'S POPULATION.

July 16, 1945- THE ATOMIC BOMB IS TESTED IN LOS ALAMOS, NM.

Aug 4, 1945- ATOMIC BOMB DROPPED ON HIROSHIMA; **80,000** KILLED.

Aug 9, 1945- SECOND ATOMIC BOMB DROPPED ON NAGASAKI.

Aug 9, 1945- RUSSIA INVADES MANCHURIA.

Sep 2, 1945- JAPAN SURRENDERS- *VJ DAY*. DURING THIS WAR, 80 MILLION SOLDIERS AND CIVILIANS HAD DIED.

Nov 29, 1947- U.N. ISSUES RESOLUTION 181- PARTITION OF PALESTINE.

May 14, 1948- ISRAELI INDEPENDENCE (YOM HA'ATZMAUT).

May 3, 1949- FALL OF SHANGHAI.

Oct 1, 1949- COMMUNIST REVOLUTION IN CHINA.

The War is Over

The war in Europe was finally over, but we did not find this out until two weeks later, as all short-wave radios had been confiscated at the start of the war. It was not until then that we heard of the atrocities perpetrated by Nazi Germany, and the willful extermination of six million Jews (of which about one quarter were from the *Auschwitz-Birkenau* camps). Rage, anguish and despair was intense as we discovered that our families and whole communities had been gassed to death and just perished off the earth.

We heard of how the Allied forces entered one death camp after another and recoiled from the horrors they had witnessed. When the BBC confirmed these reports, we were stunned. One could only imagine the anxiety of the Jewish refugees for their family members and friends who were exterminated in Europe. **How could this have happened, led by the Germans, the most cultured and technically advanced people in the world? I am convinced that if more countries, especially the United States, had allowed these Jews to enter, we would not have had the Holocaust.**

Our news of the war's progress had only been what the Japanese informed us. So, it was a great surprise to us, when on July 17, 1945, the U.S. Army Air Force bombed Shanghai with (25) A-26 bombers, carrying 100 pound bombs, centered on the *Chiang Wan Airfield*, north of Shanghai. Whilst my mother and I attended our friend *Ilse DeJong's* birthday party. The sky was severely overcast, so a few of the bombs dropped too early hitting Hongkew instead. It was mistakenly thought that their target was a Japanese radio station, but that was not so. Several hundred of the Jewish refugees, and thousands of Chinese were killed or wounded. From that day on, there was almost a daily bombardment by B-17 *Flying Fortresses* and P-40 *Flying Tigers*. For weeks the bombing continued with quiet spells between. Morale among the refugees was as low as it had ever been. We thought to ourselves, we had survived the Nazis, the Japanese; will we now be killed by the Americans, our Alies? This is what my father wrote in my diary:

"The year 1945 brought us the climax of our sufferings but also the end. Daily bombardments of Shanghai (by the Americans) were no pleasure! Prices for food soared from day to day. Very often your father had to stand on night-watch in the wee hours, whether hot or cold, and even while it was pouring rain. But all this was quickly forgotten when I got a phone call that the preliminaries of a Japanese surrender had started, and this meant the end of the war, and peace was near at hand.

My heart had always beat faster whenever I heard the Allied planes flying overhead, followed by the whistling of falling bombs; and then, finally relief when the 'all-clear' siren was heard. On Aug 6, 1945, the Atom bomb was dropped over Hiroshima, followed by Nagasaki; (which was a mere 500 miles from Shanghai).

Towards the end of the war, the U.S. Intelligence found that the Japanese were hiding their munitions within the walls of the *Ward Road Jail,* in violation of the Geneva Conference. Also, this was where the refugees sought shelter within the prison grounds. Because of this, the U.S. Army Air Force dropped leaflets warning us to keep away, that the prison would be bombed on Aug 24, but many believed it was only Japanese propaganda. (Fortunately, the war ended nine days before that dreaded scheduled date).

To announce that America was indeed winning the war, the Bank of China printed a ¥200 note, and hidden on it's face was in small type (shown in the circles) '**U S A**'.

On Aug 15th 1945 *Emperor Hirohito* finally surrendered marking the end of the war. I clearly remember when my father received a phone call from his partner in Harbin, in the middle of the night, letting him know that the war was finally over. The end was not officially reported until three days later; when we ran through the streets, crying and embracing each other. Shanghai was overwhelmed with joy. This year had brought us the height of our sufferings, but also the end.

After The War

With the end of the war, came the American GIs and their K-Rations, which could be bought on the black-market. This was when, for the first time, I tasted butter (but actually margarine with the texture of rubber, colored yellow supplied with a capsule). I remember how excited my parents were to get this stuff. Around Passover we tried to smear it on *matzos*, which I found impossible to do. However, we now could buy chocolate bars, tins of cooked chicken, instant coffee, canned milk, etc. My mother sewed me a jacket (from a pair of her ski-pants) and added U.S. military badges, which I wore with great pride.

The Japanese and *Pao Chia* were now gone. The Ghetto had ceased to exist. But, as the Japanese left Shanghai, so went all the law and order. My blanket and mosquito-net were stolen off my bed, while I was sleeping. The bathroom sink was ripped off the walls with the water pipes still connected pouring water. Laundry was stolen off the clothes-line via a bamboo pole through an open kitchen window.

Yet, these were now happy days for me and my parents. Finally, by September 1946, we moved back to the French Concession, into a beautiful 14 story hi-rise apartment house, the *Willow Court* on *#34 Route Boissezon*. I also started going to my new school, the *Shanghai Jewish School*, where I played soccer and boxed. I was driven to school each day by my friend *Mark Samuels'* chauffeur. My grades were excellent but I was often reprimanded for talking too much. This is what my father wrote in my diary:

"1946 was the most happy years for you, and for your parents. In school you started working with interest, and was always among the best of your class. You joined BETAR and become a devoted member there. In sports you were quite good- you learned to roller-skate, to ride a bike, and swimming too. But the most exciting of all was boxing, at which you showed a good fighting spirit, a lot of courage and a good fist".

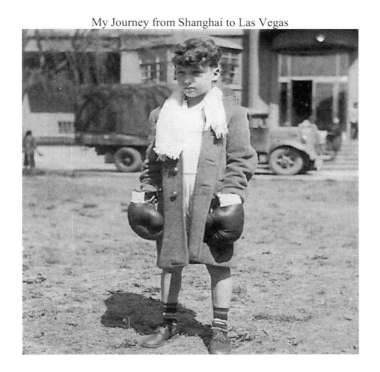

I joined *BETAR* (founded by *Joseph Trumpeldor* and *Zev Jabotinsky*), a Jewish Zionist organization similar to the Boy-scouts. On Feb 29th 1948, I won my first boxing bout against *Charlie Chan* (was that really his name?). I still have the silver cup that I had won that day.

STORY: My father was lenient, but my mother was extremely strict. She frequently hit me with her wooden (stirring) spoon. Once, she slapped me so hard across my head that her topaz ring cracked.

As kids, we played Hunters and Savages (similar to Cowboys and Indians). One day my friend *Leo* threw a bamboo spear into my head, through my pith helmet. I still have a scar there. I also liked playing with tin soldiers and loved building models.

The next summer, my family and I traveled on holiday to the mountains and beaches of *Tsingtao,* a famous resort built by the Germans in the '20s. (still famous for it's beer).

Life became very enjoyable. My parents were members of the *Jewish Recreation Club,* and the *International Shanghai Club* (located on the *Bund*), where I learned to swim and box. My parents and I often visited the *Yuen Gardens*, a most beautiful and peaceful garden and the *Public Gardens*, located along the *Bund*, beside the *Whangpoa River* adjacent to the *Soochow Creek*.

Inflation of the local currency became rampart, money was carried around in bundles and suitcases, as it's value decreased every day. (I still have a 50,000 ¥uan note then worth less than US $1.00). A pair of shoes costs two million ¥uan. A Chinese person earning three million ¥uan was starving, yet one could dine at the finest restaurant for only US $3.00. Inflation was horrendous, finally, the Nationalist government issued new currency, one gold ¥uan was equal to three million old ¥uan.

After the war was over, we found beggars everywhere, often pitifully deformed. Some, legless, sitting on wooden platforms with tiny wheels; others, blind, led by little boys; some eating bark off the trees as their only means of sustenance. To this day, I cannot leave any food on my plate!

STORY: One day my mother and I traveled to do some shopping, when she remembered that she had forgotten to shut off the stove where she had been cooking some lentils. We quickly returned to find that the pressure-cooker had exploded, our frightened Amah hiding on the balcony, and the kitchen walls covered purple.

This is what my father wrote in my diary:

"1949 was a happy year for all of us...but, many of our friends made preparations to leave Shanghai, it was time to go. In fact, the community of Jewish refugees had already started it's process of liquidation, many having left as early as '46 when the first boats became available Visa. The Civil war in China for the most part was fought in Northern China, but came nearer to Shanghai. We registered with the American Consulate.

However, your grandfather died suddenly while in New York. That was a great shock to all of us. He survived the holocaust, two concentration camps; and was eagerly looking forward to seeing his only grandchild, and hoped for a happy reunion, after these terrible years of separation.

Conditions in Shanghai became chaotic, especially with the fall of Nanking. Surely Shanghai is to be next. Normal conditions did return for a while but business came to complete standstill because the port of Shanghai was blockaded by the Nationalists. We finally received our Visas for the U.S.A., but had to wait until a steamer became available. We sold our home at a ridiculously low price, and made ourselves ready for a quick departure".

Finally, my parents felt it was time to leave for the United States, as the Communists were progressing South. It was only a matter of time before they would reach Shanghai. Enroute, the Nationalist army kept dwindling as many soldiers switched sides. The Communist soldiers were mostly teenagers, with poorly fitted uniforms, no helmets, and wearing sneakers. We appealed to my mother's sister *Hertha Saenger* and her brother *Max Kahn,* to sponsor us to come to the U.S.. They agreed, and in November we proceeded to file the immigration documents as *Stateless Refugees* with the American Consulate.

It was only then that we learnt about the horrors of the Holocaust that swept throughout Europe. We anxiously read the newspaper *Aufbau*; that's where we found out who had survived and who didn't. It was incomprehensible to believe that six million Jews were exterminated, of which 1½ million were children, half the Jews of Europe.

50

In May, the Communist army crossed the Yangtze river and entered Shanghai; once again we were faced with an uncertain future. Conditions became chaotic as we heard of their atrocities done to the Chinese. Would we now endure another Stalingrad? Fortunately, the 'Fall' of Shanghai lasted only for three hours. The currency was devalued again and the next morning a peaceful transfer of power took place. Pictures of *Chiang Kai-Shek* were quickly replaced with *Mao Zedong, Lenin* and *Marx*. On Oct 1, 1949- the *Kuomintang* (Chinese National party) capitulated, and retreated to Taiwan; China was now COMMUNIST. A few months later, the U.S. Consulate office closed, but the JDC continued to help with those having the proper documents to immigrate to the U.S.

After 10½ years in Shanghai; on Oct 29th 1949 we finally departed via the *S.S. General Gordon* (a U.S. military troop transport) holding 1,800 refugees. We had to sleep with 300 men, or women, in the cargo-holds of the ship, in triple bunk-beds (I slept on the top bunk).

STORY: Enroute I threw up a tape-worm onto the guy who's bunk was below mine; he was not very happy. I also had an accident aboard when I hit my head running on the steel deck floor and lost consciousness. This trip was grueling, my father told me to pretend that I was in the Navy; yet I was seasick for 18 of the 19 day journey.

Years later, in March 2009, I made and published a 38 minute movie *"My Shanghai Memoirs"*, which was this story told on film. It was edited by our friend *Abe Schwartz*, who had been a professional videographer. The film is now archived at the *'Yad Vashem Library of the Diaspora'*.

To acknowledge those who lived in and survived the Shanghai Ghetto, a wall with 13,700 former refugee names were engraved. (paid for by contributions from the *Spungen* Organization). See my name above...

Article

On October 27, 2017 I was interviewed by *Kevin Ostoyich*, history professor of the Valparaiso University, who wrote and published the following article. I have attached some excerpts of this article:

[7] "THE STORY OF BERT REINER, THE TOY MAKER, APPRECIATION OF THE EXPERIENCES OF FORMER SHANGHAI JEWISH REFUGEES.

During the 1983 Christmas season, Coleco Industries, Inc. took the world by storm with a novel concept for a doll: Each doll was unique and would be adopted by a child. Reports started to pop up of parents fighting—even trampling—each other in order to get the individualized dolls for their children. A Christmas sensation swept through the land. Every kid wanted to 'adopt' their unique Cabbage Patch Kid. The concept of a mass-produced doll based on each being uniquely different posed a challenge for the engineers in charge of the production. It was one thing to mass produce figures or dolls that were identical; it was entirely different to mass produce dolls that were all different -- varied by face, eye color, hair color, hair style, and the like. This was the challenge for the toy maker, Bert Reiner.

In the office of his Las Vegas home, Bert has a framed copy of *Newsweek*. On the cover is a little girl kissing a red-headed, blue-eyed doll under the title, 'What a Doll! The Cabbage Patch Craze.' Seventy years earlier, Bert's parents had very different concerns than purchasing a doll for their son. In December 1943 Bert and his parents were living in the Designated Area, known as the 'Shanghai Ghetto,' that had been set up by the occupying Japanese forces in Shanghai. The Ghetto was located in the poorest section of a city known for its rampant disease, squalor, and poor sanitation. The conditions may have been deplorable, but children found ways to adapt and play.

For Bert and his friends, even cigarette packs were fair game—they folded them into small squares that they flipped in a game called 'Packs,' similar to 'Marbles,' another favorite of the refugee children in Shanghai. The children also tried their luck in a popular knock-off of 'Monopoly' called 'Shanghai Millionaire.' The refugees living in the Ghetto were anything but millionaires. Nevertheless, despite the restricted nature of their existence, they were fortunate in comparison to those friends and relatives who had not joined them in their journeys to Shanghai.

The Reiners were from Dresden, Germany, and like approximately 18,000 other Jewish refugees, they had fled to Shanghai to escape the clutches of Hitler's Nazi regime. Bert's paternal grandfather owned a department store in the city called 'Kaufhaus Reiner.' Bert's father, Horst, who had been born in Dresden, worked in his father's department store for a while. He graduated from the university and then went on to work in the import/export business, primarily in pharmaceuticals and chemicals used in the perfume industry. Bert describes his father as a 'very brilliant' man who had a photographic memory and was proficient in thirteen languages, of which he was fluent in six. More importantly, Bert remembers his father as having been his best friend. His mother was from Frankfurt, had five siblings, and was a homemaker.

Bert's parents had met at a masquerade party. They had had a child before Bert, but there were complications with the birth, and the child passed away after four months. Bert was born in Dresden in 1937. Horst named his boy after his best friend Norbert Strier.

During the following year, the persecution of the Jews in Germany reached a new level. On 'Kristallnacht' of November 9-10, 1938, Jewish-owned businesses, residences, and synagogues were vandalized and destroyed. Horst's best friend, Norbert Strier, who had been to Shanghai before and thought it a good haven, suggested that they all go to Shanghai (which was the only port not requiring a visa). At first, Horst declined, feeling Germany was his rightful home. Ultimately, after Kristallnacht, however, he came to the realization that it would be best for the family to leave, and he entrusted Norbert Strier with all his money to invest in behalf of the Reiner family.

The family purchased a forty-foot wood container called a *'Lift'* in order to hold all their furniture and belongings. As with other Jews who were fleeing the country, the Reiners were only allowed to leave Germany with 10 Marks per person.

The family left Germany from Bremerhaven on the Norddeutscher Lloyd luxury liner, SS *Potsdam,* in March 1939. The ship traveled to Genoa, Italy, through the Suez Canal, and then stopped in Kobe, Japan. The Reiner's contemplated staying in Kobe, where there were a number of other Jews, but decided to continue on to Hong Kong and ultimately Shanghai.

Upon arriving in Shanghai, they moved into a house in the French Concession, which was the nicest neighborhood in the city. Unfortunately, Horst contracted spinal meningitis soon thereafter, and was not expected to survive. Trudy thus found herself with a toddler, a gravely ill husband, and in a foreign land where she did not know the language. She went to Norbert Strier to ask about their money entrusted to him, and learned that it was all gone. Making matters worse, not a trace of the jewelry she had requested to have hidden in the Reiner furniture could be found. Fortunately, Horst survived the bout with meningitis. Nevertheless, Horst and Trudy resolved never to speak to Norbert Strier ever again. From then on there was only to be one Bert in their lives.

Aboard ship, Horst had become acquainted with Fritz Wolf, and later Max Fleischmann. Fleischmann was already established in China and lived most of his time in Harbin, Manchuria. Together, the three men created an import/export

55

company called the *Fleischmann Impex Company*. In the period before the Japanese bombed Pearl Harbor and seized control of Shanghai, Horst conducted business on behalf of the company. But then, the war put a freeze on the import/export trade and the company lay dormant as a result. Horst then shifted his focus to helping Jewish organizations secure money and food for the Kitchen Fund, upon which many refugees depended for their sustenance.

The Reiners continued to live comfortably in the French Concession until the Japanese issued a proclamation which stipulated that all stateless refugees who had entered after January 1, 1937, had to move into a Designated Area (the Shanghai Ghetto) in Hongkew. Fortunately, Horst's business partner, Fleischmann, owned a villa in Hongkew, and the Reiners were able to move in there. Fleischmann's house was divided among four families. The Wolfs and the Reiners lived on the first floor and two Polish Jewish refugee families lived on the second floor. Most other refugees were crammed into abysmal living quarters within the Ghetto.

The family employed 'amahs' (servants) throughout their entire time they lived in Shanghai. The amahs served as nannies for Bert. Both of his parents were very busy in Shanghai. While living in the Ghetto, Trudy cooked for those who were less fortunate in a charity Kitchen. Although their living arrangements were better than those of most refugees, they were not without problems and worries. Horst was not able to work; thus, they did not have any income. Given they had brought from Germany a lot of furniture and personal belongings (including crystal, silverware, and china), they started to sell their possessions and live off the proceeds. Although they employed amahs, Trudy always did her own cooking.

Bert remembers growing up having European food rather than Chinese food. They rarely had meat. Conditions in the Ghetto were rather bleak and the future uncertain.

56

Bert notes that while in Shanghai, his mother had an abortion, not wanting another child at that time. Most of their friends either had one child or none.

Horst often needed to go outside of the Ghetto and thus needed to get a pass. Sometimes he got it, sometimes he did not. Overall, however, he did not encounter too many problems. Perhaps this was due to Horst's diminutive stature. *Kanoh Ghoya*, (the unstable and often sadistic Japanese official who oversaw the distribution of the passes), was an extremely short man and did not take kindly to tall men, often slapping and humiliating them.

The school where Bert attended in the Ghetto was the Shanghai Jewish Youth Association School, which was also known as the Kadoorie School after its Sephardic Jewish benefactor, Sir Horace Kadoorie. After the war he attended the Shanghai Jewish School. He remembers the quality of instruction at both schools being very high. He says he did well in both schools and has a report card that indicates that he was first in his class but also reprimanded him for talking too much. When it came to schoolwork, Horst was always a great help to him. Bert did not participate very much in sports but did play soccer and swam, his father having taught him the latter. Bert also liked to box. Bert did not attend a separate Hebrew school, but Hebrew was part of the curriculum of both the schools.

Bert describes his parents as not having been very religious. Horst came from a family in which his father was Jewish, but his mother was not. Although Trudy had come from a religious household, she herself was not. Bert remembers how when they lived in the Fleischmann Villa, the two Polish Jewish families on the second floor were Orthodox and kept kosher, whereas on the first floor the Reiner family did not.

The Reiners did observe holidays, but they did not attend synagogue on a regular basis. Bert notes that his level of religiosity remained pretty much the same after the family arrived in the United States. In the years since, the only major change for Bert was that when he married his wife, Sandy, he agreed to keep kosher at their home, to honor the wishes of her father.

Bert remembers only being with other German, Austrian, and Polish Jews friends, and after the war he did have some interaction with Russian Jews. Bert's best friend was a Russian immigrant. His friend's father actually had a car with a driver (which was very unusual). They picked Bert up every morning and drove him to school. Bert does not remember any interactions with any British or Americans.

Initially, Bert had an ambivalent attitude toward the Americans, for they had bombed the Ghetto in July 1945. He quickly overcame these reservations after the war, however, and started to look up to the American soldiers. Trudy took a pair of her ski pants and made a jacket for Bert with American military badges sewn; Bert wore this jacket with pride.

Overall, Bert believes life after the war was good in Shanghai. The family moved into a nice fourteen-story apartment house back into the French Concession, Horst resumed work in the import/export business with Europe and the United States, and Bert started to attend the Shanghai Jewish School. Bert remembers that living was very comfortable, but that would not last. The Communists were closing in. When the Communists took over the country on October 1, 1949, Horst and Trudy decided it was time to leave. Given they had family sponsors and the quota was high for Germans wanting to enter the U.S. they did not have difficulty securing the visa.

The family left Shanghai on October 29, 1949, on the troop transporter, the USS *General W. H. Gordon*. Bert slept in the hold of the overcrowded ship with 300 men in triple bunks. He proceeded to get seasick for 18 of the 19 days of the voyage. He also had a serious accident in which he hit his head on the steel deck floor and lost consciousness. All things told, it was not a pleasant voyage for the twelve-year-old. They arrived in San Francisco, where they stayed for three weeks, then they took a train to New York City.

At school, Bert was put into a class that corresponded with his age (twelve). Nevertheless, the level of instruction in Shanghai had been so high that he felt that he was much more advanced than his classmates. Bert eventually attended Brooklyn Tech and had to commute via subway each day from Queens. He did not participate in sports or other activities, focusing instead on his studies. Overall, he believes he received an excellent education.

Bert remembers learning about the horrors of the Holocaust through the newspaper *Aufbau* in New York. People read the newspaper continuously to find out who survived and who didn't, and it was a continuous shock. It was hard to believe. Throughout the war they had no idea what was going on in Europe. Trudy had come from a family of six children. She had had a brother who had passed away but whose death was not related to the Holocaust. Another brother had a wife with family living in the United States and moved there. One of her sisters moved to New York with her husband. Another sister as a Zionist moved to Israel. Trudy's father and her youngest sister stayed in Germany and were ultimately killed in a concentration camp in Poland. It was not until a few years ago, when Bert visited *Yad Vashem* (the World Holocaust Remembrance Center in Jerusalem), that he was able to find out where and when his grandfather and aunt were killed.

Horst's mother, sister, and brother-in-law stayed in Dresden and survived the war. Horst's mother was Lutheran but converted to Judaism, but when the war started she converted back to Christianity and was thus able to survive. Horst's father, on the other hand, was Jewish and was sent first to *Sachsenhausen* and then *Theresienstad* concentration camps. He survived the war and came to the United States.

After graduating from Brooklyn Tech, Bert went to college at Rensselaer Polytechnic Institute in Troy, New York. It was there that he met his wife, Sandy. He started his career at Sikorsky Aircraft, then took a job at Sound Scriber, then with several toy companies: A.C. Gilbert, Ideal Toy, and Coleco Industries, Inc. Since June 1988, he has served as the president of his own company, 'Reiner Associates, Inc', which does consulting work for the toy industry.

In 2009 Bert created a DVD about his Shanghai experience titled *'My Shanghai Memoirs'*. He says, *"It was primarily for our children and grandchildren so that they would understand and appreciate my experiences."* Since making the DVD, he has been asked to speak about Shanghai publicly in both Connecticut and Las Vegas, presenting to various Jewish and genealogy groups. Bert researched the topic for about a year before making the film. He started reading many of the memoirs that had been written by survivors and he watched some of the documentaries.

When Bert completed his Bar Mitzvah, Horace presented him with the book and a bicycle: *"At thirteen years old that book held no interest for me. It was only the bicycle. However, that bike had rusted and is long gone; but that book I still cherish."*

Kevin continues to interview people who had survived the Shanghai Ghetto, he will eventually write a book about his findings and research.

We've Arrived

After departing Shanghai, we traveled to Hong Kong, Yokohama, Hawaii, but could not depart onto U.S. soil until we reached San Francisco. During this journey I ate nothing but apples. This was the first time I ever ate fresh fruit without having to peel it first. We were overwhelmed with gratitude when we saw at last, the beautiful *Golden Gate Bridge* gleaming in the sunshine.

We first arrived at *Angel Island* in San Francisco, were quickly processed, then spent three weeks visiting old friends from Shanghai. We, then traveled cross-country by train, arriving in New York City on Armistice Day (November 11, 1949). Upon our arrival, we stayed briefly at my aunt *Hertha* and uncle *Ho*'s apartment in Manhattan, near the Fort Tryon Park, whilst the apartment building in *Kew Garden Hills* was being built. While there, I went to school at PS 117, and found that I was way ahead of the other students in my classes.

STORY: My mother and I traveled by subway to Queens (our first trip) to see the progress of the apartment being built, which was to be our new home. As I stood there admiring the train, the doors closed-- my mother in the subway, and I still left on the platform.

I found it difficult to leave my friends in Shanghai, start to make new friends in Manhattan, and now to start over again in Queens. Given that I spoke English with a British accent, I tended to pronounce words such as aluminum "*aloo-mee-nium*", the kids often laughed at me.

STORY: Shortly after we arrived, several girls (as a joke) invited me to their Pajama Party. I was too shy to go, but my mother urged me, saying "*I must do what the American kids do*". When I arrived at the girl's home, they all giggled; and very, very embarrassed, I walked home.

Eventually, I did make friends and settled into our new home in Queens. My closest friends in high school were *Gordon Saks* (later became CFO of *Harry N. Abrams Publishers*, then CEO of *Lion Press*), *Ronny Lissman* (later became owner of *Lisco Trading* company importer of sardines) and *John Romano* (became a gangster), and my girlfriend *Shirley Hazan* (became a model).

QUOTE: "Those who cannot remember the past, are condemned to repeat it". *Georg Santayana*

Part 2

The Fifties

(1950 - 1960)

At Brooklyn Tech

I applied to, and was admitted to the auspicious *Brooklyn Technical High* school, in Brooklyn, NY, where I commuted 1¼ hours each way, via subway from/to Queens.

STORY: While in high school, I got into a number of hijinks. My classmate *John Romano*, had (accidently) stabbed me in my arm while playing with his switch-blade knife on the desk. On one day, the captain of the gym team and I had a food fight in the cafeteria, then continued outside after school. He won. I left with my left eye bleeding and completely closed and was immediately rushed to an ophthalmic surgeon. Fortunately my eye sight was intact. The next day, for revenge, my friend Romano beat him up.

My closest friend growing up with me in Shanghai was *Marc Samuels*. Because he and his mother were both born in China, they found it difficult to imigrate to the U.S. They came here on a visitor's visa but when it expired, they never left. Marc got Leukemia, and on July 16, 1953, jumped from the 7th floor of the Sloan Kettering Hospital to his death, while his parents were downstairs about to visit him.

STORY: While on a double-date, Romano 'borrowed' a NY City Garbage Truck (which he obtained showing his ID from where he worked as a N.Y. City lifeguard); we used it to go with our dates to the movies.

STORY: In my junior year at Brooklyn Tech I took a Printing class which involved writing a paragraph, selecting lead type from a 'California type' case, then mounting it onto a 'Composing stick', then printing on a printing press, to be approved. We worked in pairs, and I was much faster than my partner, I gave him my finished printed paragraph, got caught, and we both flunked the class.

STORY: I had a tropical fresh-water fish tank; and I would also buy and sell fish to our friends. I prepared a catalogue, bought the fish at a fish breeder, and sold them at retail. One time my best friend *Gordon Saks* and I poisoned *Paul Sturm's* tropical fish because we were jealous that he had more expensive fish than we could afford. I saved all my dead fish, every time one of my fish died, I preserved it. Eventually, I had more preserved dead fish, than in the tank.

In May, I had my *Bar Mitzvah* at the *Jewish Center of Kew Gardens*. For that occasion, I received two gifts from my parents: a bicycle and a diary of my life in Shanghai (which my father spent several months preparing). I looked forward to my bicycle, but did not appreciate the latter. Now, however, the bike is rusted and long gone, but that diary is always cherished. On the first page my father wrote:

"My dear son, your parents are presenting you on the occasion of your Bar Mitzvah with this book, which is much more than an album. In fact it should show you something of the family you are coming from – pictures and documents of you and our life. Keep it close to your heart and wherever you might choose to go in the days ahead, remember your parents who brought you up with the wish to keep away from you harm,

become an upright man, loyal citizen of the USA and faithful as a Jew. This is the wish of your loving parents.

It is almost unbelievable for us, that our son Norbert is already maturing to be a man, as our Jewish religion prescribes for boys of 13 years. We have held many pleasant memories to date, but it is impossible to reproduce them in such a book as this. We are dedicating this book to you on the day of your Bar Mitzvah, it's a sketch, a brief outline of your life during these past 13 years. But, many sad memories were not recorded here, as it is our wish that you should remember only the happy days of your childhood. Remember, my son, to link you're Jewish traditions with your life here in America. Be ever ready to learn, be tolerant, be broadminded. Do well, whatever you do, achievement is the only enduring satisfaction in life.

With all our love, *your parents*".

In high school, my first job was delivering newspapers, the *Long Island Daily Press.* I won a three day trip to Williamsburg, VA and Annapolis, MD for selling subscriptions. At home, my mother spoke primarily German, knowing very little English before coming to the U.S. After we arrived, however, my father anglicized his name from *Horst* to *Horace*, and persuaded my mother to only read books and newspapers in English. Whenever she started to revert back to speaking German, my father would use our code word *'switch'*, meaning she should switch back to English.

I also held several jobs: delivering (and assisting with filling prescriptions) at *Belle Drug Store;* bus-boy at *Monsey Park Hotel;* dance instructor at *Dale Dance Studio;* counselor at *Boy Scout Camp*; delivering telegrams for *Western Union* on Wall Street; lifeguard at *Tumbleweed Ranch* in the Catskills; and head-waiter at *Goldman Hotel* in Orange, NJ.

My best friend through high school and college, was *Gordon Sakoloff*. While I worked at the pharmacy, I once broke some thermometers so I could play with Mercury (Gordon's idea). We did everything together, including stealing a tuxedo we each used while working as a waiter. He later went to a federal prison for cheating on a SBA loan. Gordon was the only one of my friends that had a TV (14" screen), so we spent a lot of time together.

STORY: Although my primary job at *Tumbleweed Ranch* was as their lifeguard, I was also given several other tasks, including carrying out the garbage, shoeing horses (got kicked in the head, narrowly missing my eye), and checking the chlorine level for the water-supply. During the one day that I forgot to check the water, a County Health Inspector came to find that the chlorine level had dropped to '0'. The Inspector threatened to close the camp, but settled for my being fired.

STORY: I also worked on my cousin *Walter Kahn's* chicken farm. I not only collected eggs every day, I also had the job of catching 'chicken peckers.' These were chickens that would peck on the rear of another chicken, making it bleed. When caught, we would drill a hole in their beaks (it didn't hurt), then attach metal blinders which allowed them to look down to eat, but not straight ahead: problem solved.

STORY: At one visit to my uncle's, Walter and I were going to the movies. He had just gotten his driver's license that day. I was bugging him to the point that he got so annoyed that he pulled over and threw me out of the truck. Here I was on a dark highway, in an unknown area somewhere in New Jersey, so I started to walk. I finally stopped at a nearby farmhouse and persuaded the people to drive me back to my uncle's. When Walter returned several hours later (my uncle hid me to teach his son a lesson), Walter assumed that I was there, but his parents said I wasn't, Walter got hysterical.

I joined the Boy Scouts, and quickly became an Eagle Scout with a Silver Palm, and went to Scout camps at *Alpine*, NJ, and *Ten Mile River*, NY. My Eagle Scout award was presented to me by *Vladimir Zworykin*, the inventor of the television CRT tube (without which we would not have TV today). While at camp I was initiated into the *Order Of The Arrow*, (Indian folk dancing). The initiation required being silent for three days, with a carved wood arrow in my mouth. During my last summer at scout-camp, I attended a sea-scout camp, (only for Explorer scouts); where we lived on a 'land-secured' ship.

STORY: One weekend (when families were visiting), I installed speakers and microphones in the latrine. When a young girl would go to sit on a 'hole', I would say (from the outside), *"hay lady, please move, I am painting down here"*.

STORY: When I was a counselor at the *Ten-Mile-River Scout* camp, I took a group on an extended hike, and got lost. I was following red dots (painted can tops) which were posted along the trail;, but it got so dark I eventually could no longer see them. We then stopped and made camp for the night. But, we were not prepared for an overnight trip; we had no tents, no flashlights, no food, and I was responsible for 12 scared scouts.

STORY: Later, as an Explorer scout leader, I took the group to *Powder Ridge Mountain,* in Middlefield, CT, to teach them skiing, despite never having skied myself. After putting on our ski equipment, we each got on the ski lift, and then waited for the lift to stop to let us off (I did not know that the lift never stops, that we needed to jump off). Finally, before crashing into the end as the lift swings around, the operator realized we were in trouble, did shut it off and he screamed *"who is in charge?"*

67

STORY: I always wanted to learn to blow a bugle; on my fifteenth birthday, my parents and I went to buy one. In the store, I tried to blow, and blow, and blow, but no sound came out. That was the end of my musical career.

While waiting at a bus stop near our home in Forest Hills, a man suddenly fell down and went into an epileptic seizure. I went to his aide, put my wallet in his mouth, and covered him with my coat till the ambulance arrived. Having saved his life, onlookers were shouting **"hero"**.

On one of our dates, *Shirley Hazen* and I went to dinner in the city. When we returned to the parking lot, the car wasn't there— It had been stolen! The car was recovered the next day, but boy did I get HELL.

STORY: While on a double-date with Shirley and her friend *Ann Sue Moskowitz*, I drove first to pick up Ann Sue; but had a difficult time parking, ending up on the side-walk. Her father saw how and where I parked, called Shirley's father and told him not to let me drive!

At my graduation from Brooklyn Tech, our senior prom was held at the *Waldorf Astoria*; followed by a ride on the Staten Island Ferry; my date was *Shirley Hazen*.

STORY: My parents celebrated their 25th wedding anniversary in Florida, while I stayed behind. So, this was my opportunity to 'borrow' my father's car. Without a license, not being experienced with a manual-shift (1951 Chevy), I stalled while trying to cross the *Horace Harding Boulevard* enroute to a movie. A policeman pushed my car (without my having a drivers license), across the busy intersection.

There are hundreds of other stories from my time in New York, but that would take another book to cover it all.

68

At Rensselaer

After my graduation from Brooklyn Tech, I went to *Rensselaer Polytechnic Institute* (RPI), in Troy, NY., graduating in June 1960 with a BME. I did reasonably well, my only weak class was in Thermodynamics. I was president of *Alpha Phi Omega* (AΦΩ Service fraternity), active in *Hillel Club*, and also *Tau Epsilon Phi* (TEΦ Social fraternity). During my Freshman year, I lived in the dorms and worked serving food at the dining hall (which I did for all four years). I also played soccer on the varsity team. During my Sophomore year I lived in the upper-class dorms, then an apartment in my Junior year, and the TEΦ fraternity house in my Senior year.

STORY: One night, while serving food in the cafeteria, I cut my finger on the sharp edges of the stainless-steel pans, getting blood all over the chicken-a-la-king. What should I do? I stirred the blood around, and no one noticed.

My father died during my Sophomore year at RPI and it was no longer financially feasible for me to continue my education there. That Summer, I got a job at *Grumman Aircraft* in Bethpage, LI. My title was 'Apprentice Engineer,' but my job was actually drilling (millions) of holes into aircraft wings. After six months I'd had enough, and enrolled at *Pratt Institute*. Both Brooklyn Tech and RPI were all boy schools, but Pratt was mostly girls- I really liked that! But the education was not the same, so, after completing one semester, I went back to RPI on a limited scholarship. At times, I had as many as five jobs to pay for my tuition, as my mother was not able to help.

STORY: Being the youngest person working at Grumman, I was often the butt of my co-worker's jokes. They had me go to the tool-shed to get a 'foot of assembly-line', or painted '**7**' on the back of my shoes (like I stole them from a bowling alley), and nailed my seat onto the floor.

69

I had worked as a waiter at *Kiamisha Lake Country Club* (1958), and *Cavitron Dental* in Long Island City (1959).

STORY: I worked each Summer as a waiter in the Catskills. During one summer, I met and dated *Violet Sass* (cousin to *Zsa Zsa Gabor*), who was married with a child and was cheating on her husband, with me. During his visit, he found out, and threatened me to have me marry her. He returned to the city, and we resumed our affair.

My goal was to make a lot of money, so I did everything I could to maximize my tips: I gave extra deserts, served breakfast after the kitchen closed, etc. However, on one occasion I got a lousy tip from a wife after taking care of her family of three for a whole week. So I apologized for giving them 'poor service', they were so embarrassed that I promptly got another tip from her husband.

On December 18, 1955 I became a U.S. Citizen.

70

STORY: I took my driving test in Queens, but flunked. Later, while at RPI I retried the exam. This time my sister-in-law *Phyllis* (who was 7 months pregnant) sat in the back seat; the examiner thought that she was my wife-- I passed.

Sandy and I had great times at the various 'frat' parties, dancing and drinking (screwdrivers, 7+7, sloe-gin-fizz). Girls were not allowed above the 1st floor (things have changed since then). We played 45rpm records (that's before CDs) and danced through the nights.

I joined TEΦ in my Junior year. For our initiation, the pledges had to measure the distance around the campus. This did not seem too difficult until we found out we had to measure the campus with a HERRING. We took a (precise) 10" herring and laid it end-to-end along the streets. Can you imagine the ensuing smell as it got warmer?

STORY: We had very icy winters in Troy, and in my Junior year the apartment I lived in had a severe hill. Sometime during the night someone hit my parked car and dented the rear. After we exchanged info, I went back to sleep. Two hours later, I got hit again (in the same spot); got money from both insurance companies!

STORY: My landlord during this year was quite obese and could not fit into the shower we shared, so she began to smell badly. On top of that, she never cleaned the bathroom. One day I brought some *Potassium Permanganate* (dark purple crystals) from the chemistry lab and sprinkled them all over the floor. Knowing the crystals would turn red when mixed with water, I was hoping she would at least mop the floors! But, rather than cleaning up, she accused a 90 year old tenant of having her period and dripping blood onto the floor. Finally she called the Fire Department, believing were rats in the basement. She never did mop the floor! RPI was good for my family, my brother-in-law Bill and Eric all went there.

71

We're Married

During my sophomore year at RPI, I met my future wife *Sandra Jay Winkler,* who was born and raised in Troy, NY. Sandy and I met at USY where I was an advisor. I liked her from the start, she was pretty, pleasant, outspoken and busty (all the attributes I liked). She was only 14 when we started to date (I was 18). Two years later, on April 28, 1958, we were pinned (TEΦ) at the *Knotty Pine* restaurant.

As I was dating Sandy, I spent a lot of my time at the Winkler's (sometimes instead of studying). We both spent a lot of time on the farm of *Marvin* (died September 2, 2005), *Judy,* and *Howard Ginsburg.* Once, while I was trying to ride a tractor, I almost ran over cousin Howard.

The following year, on 1959 New Year's Eve, we became engaged while in New York City. We were married shortly after my graduation, on June 25, 1960, at *Beth El Synagogue*, with the reception following at the *Masonic Temple*, in Troy, NY. *Gordon Saks* was my best-man, and Sandy's cousin *Susan Pozefsky* was her Maid-of-Honor,

STORY: Earlier in the day of our wedding, Gordon and I went to the *Hendrick Hudson* hotel to have some pre-wedding drinks. While there, we met the dishwasher from the RPI dining room, sitting at the bar. Gordon invited him to my wedding. He had a great time and can be seen in every one of our pictures.

Two cups of wine are used in the wedding ceremony. The first cup accompanies the brothel blessings recited by the rabbi. Then, the *Sheva Brachot* (seven blessings) are recited, followed by the couple to drink from the second cup. Wine, a symbol of joy in Jewish tradition, is associated with *Kiddush*, the prayer recited on every Shabbat and holiday. The marriage becomes official when the groom gives an object of value to the bride, traditionally done with a ring. The groom then declares *"Behold, you are betrothed unto me with this ring."* The conclusion of the ceremony is with the tradition of the groom shattering a cloth-wrapped glass, or a flash-bulb. The marriage is than consummated.

After our wedding, we drove down to our new home in Bridgeport, CT. Enroute, driving south along the dark and winding Route 7, Sandy cried that she wanted to go be back to Troy to be with her parents. (What a way to start a marriage). We spent our honeymoon at the *Nevele Grande Hotel*, in Ellenville, NY.

STORY: We drove down to the 1965 World's Fair in Queens. While walking Leibschen (then about 4 months old), Sandy decided to save parking in front of Omi's house, and stood in an empty spot. Then a guy drove into that same spot, pushing Sandy out of the way. Getting out of his car, his wife then yelled at me, *"who do you think you are, you lousy Jew"*. I respond: *"keep your big mouth shut"*, whereupon he swings at me, misses, and hits Sandy in the eye. I then hit him, he falls and hits his head against the side of the building, is unconscious and his wife thinks he's dead, but is OK.

73

My Papi

Horace: During my Sophomore year, Sandy and I attended the Air Force ROTC ball, and on Sunday of that weekend, my parents joined us at the Dave Brubeck Concert. Unfortunately, this was the only time that Sandy had met my father. He had a photographic memory; spoke, read and could write fluently in six languages: English, German, French, Spanish, Russian and Chinese. He helped a lot of my classmates with their foreign studies homework. He was extremely honest, charitable, organized, and fastidious.

He had read the NY City subway map while we were on the boat coming to the U.S., memorizing it long before he ever saw a subway. Later, but not too soon after arriving, he often gave directions to New Yorkers. He loved children, patting every little kid he saw on the head (today he might be arrested for attempted molestation). My parents seemed to have had a good relationship; I never saw them fight or argue.

STORY: In my house growing up, my mother was the disciplinarian. My father hit me only twice that I can remember. At about age 10, I left for my friend *Mark Samuel's* house and 'forgot' to come home. When I did finally come much later, my father beat me with a coat-hanger. At another time, at about age 14, I went to the super's workshop in the *Kew Garden Hill's* basement. I forgot dinner, and my parents had called the police. This time I got a beating from my mother with a wooden spoon.

We usually ate dinner late, at about 8:00pm. My father was always catered to first, then me. If I didn't like something to eat, I was given DOUBLE. So, now I eat everything!

I remember one day, while accompanying my father to the hospital, we stopped enroute for me to ice-skate at the *Radio City Rink* while he looked on. This is a favorite memory of mine.

Early in his career, my father became seriously ill. He was diagnosed with cancer, and was treated at the *Sloan Kettering* Memorial Hospital. On March 27, 1957, at only age 50, he died of the dreadful disease *Lympho-Sarcoma Cancer*. My mother called me while I was at school and I drove down from Troy to NYC just in time to see my father pass away.

Later, as I was speaking with the Rabbi to discuss the burial details, he pointed out that as my grandmother was not Jewish I had to show evidence of my father's *Brith & Bar Mitzvah* in order to allow him to perform the funeral; fortunately I had those documents with me. He is buried at *Cedar Park Cemetery*, Paramus, NJ, near his father

QUOTE: **"If it's worth doing, then do it well"**.
Horace Reiner

75

My Momi

After my father died, my mother was still young (and pretty). She dated often. She got a job (her first job ever) as an accounting clerk at *Nationwide Insurance*. She was a great social director and loved to make parties. She was also a great cook and house-keeper. Unfortunately, my mother had her favorites of our children: Eric (who looked like me), and later it was Ari (who also looked like me). Zach once said after leaving her house, that he felt '*invisible*', which made us feel very sad.

She eventually met a man (*Mr. Mort*) whom she liked, but lived in Clifton, NJ who had proposed marriage to her. She declined, saying that she would never live in Clifton (where she did end up living there in her last dozen years).

STORY: My mother was very frugal. At the end of each 6 months period, rather than go next door to the bank to update her T-bills (they charged $25), she rode the subway plus two buses to the downtown Treasury, where it was free. But, as a precaution, in case she got mugged, she sewed the T-bills inside the lining of her coat.

STORY: In the German language, numbers are reversed. One day, she was talking to Harold's grandmother, when she told her (without realizing) she was 68 years old, but was actually 86, she did look younger, but not that young.

My mother was impeccably clean and neat and would frequently scold Sandy when she found clothes lying around our house. Because of the unsanitary conditions that we found living in China, my mother, before sitting down to eat at a new restaurant, would first inspect the kitchen. I was taught to never eat raw vegetables (that's why I don't eat salads), or drink water from the tap (only drink bottled club soda).

My mother and Sandy did not get along too well, they often fought over trivial things. The habit that irritated Sandy the most, was when my mother would feed food to our kids, using her own fork.

STORY: My mother had some larceny in her. Once, Sandy and I went to buy a couch. On display were some cushions on the couch that she felt should have been included (but weren't). When we got home, my mother opened her coat to reveal two cushions.

My mother was two years older than my father (I found this out later looking at docs after my father's death). This was considered a '*shande*' (disgrace) to her friends. So, my mother lied her entire life to make herself four years younger.

After seven years of being a widow, she married *Otto Katz*, staying in the city. Sandy, I, and the kids liked him a lot. He treated my mother well. Otto died on June 17, 1981.

Later, at age 90, Omi (as she was affectionately called by my children and grandchildren), moved into an independent living facility, the *Daughters of Miriam* in Clifton, NJ. She celebrated her 100th birthday there with her family and friends (not many were left). For her last ten years she had had an aide, *Sandra Rampersad*, who took care of her needs 24/7, never taking a day off.

STORY: When Sandra first moved in with her, we bought her a pullout day-bed for her use in the living-room. On the day of the bed's delivery, my mother called up to say that the color of the bed's arms did not match the rest of her furniture. When I refused to make a change, she threatened to tell all her friends to no longer visit her, because she was too embarrassed by the color mismatch.

As she grew older, in her late nineties, her memory was still intact. One day Sandy asked my mother her name, but she could not remember. A few minutes later, our dog Georgie was trying to get under the breakfront to retrieve his ball, when my mother said: *"Sandy, get your dog..."*.

My mother lived a long, but difficult life: she had lost her mother when she was only 12; lost her first born son (*Manfred*); witnessed the start of Nazi Germany; suffered through WW-II under Japanese occupation while in the Shanghai Ghetto; present at the invasion of Communist China; lost her husband (*Horace*); and her 2nd husband (*Otto*); yet, lived to a ripe old age of 102.

Papa Lou and Betty

Lou: Sandy's parents were great and everyone loved them, especially me. *Louis David 'Leibke' Winkler* was born in *Rodomsko*, Lodz, Poland on December 25, 1903. He, his mother, and brother arrived at Ellis Island in 1905 aboard the *RMS Carmania*. His father had imigrated two years earlier. On May 2, 1926, Lou married Betty at Washington Park in Troy, NY; and later moved to 1 Reid Avenue, also in Troy. Lou was strictly kosher and *'davened'* (prayed) daily but did allow his wife and kids to eat in non-kosher restaurants. Lou was very kind, generous, easy going (except on Saturdays when he could not smoke), and gave to every bum on the street, and to any and all Indian tribes (I don't know why he seemed to favor the Indians).

Every Rosh Hashanah, Sandy, Caryl, Marve and I, and all our children, would drive up to observe the holidays at the *Washington Hotel*, in Sharon Springs, NY. Papa Lou and I would be in the synagogue, and the ladies were off doing their thing.

79

Back in Troy we would often have dinner at *Joe's* in Albany. Of course, Papa Lou would always pay for me. One night, however, I wanted to treat, but he refused. I got so angry that I even threatened to stop seeing his daughter; finally the dispute of the bill was resolved, when Joe paid it!

On May 2, 1976, all the kids celebrated the Winkler's 50th Wedding anniversary at *Tamarack Lodge* in the Catskills, that's when Sandy (at age 36) won 1st prize in a bathing suit contest. Papa Lou and I designed and patented the 'Safety-Hanger', a hanger to support clothes during transportation.

STORY: We went to an Italian restaurant where I ate escargot. As the waiter was delivering the dinner, my plate tilted, and the snails almost 'jumped' onto Papa Lou's plate.

STORY: Nana Betty's hobby was making ceramics. She made a beautiful, blue, antique lamp for us. Unfortunately, it didn't fit in our modern home's decor. I made this known to Papa Lou, whereupon he became very insulted, packed up, and left for home. We did keep however, and cherished, a ceramic white Cat which we keep in our LV home, and a multi-colored ceramic Rooster in our CT home.

STORY: Driving enroute to Troy, I would tell our kids stories from the Bible, or their favorite story of 'Falling Rock'…. *"There once was an Indian maiden who was in love with a young warrior named Falling Rock, but so was another warrior White Stallion. In order to select who would marry her, the maiden's father decided to have each warrior go out into the forest; whomever would return after 10 days with the largest number of animal skins, would win his daughter in marriage. After 10 days, White Stallion returned with 12 beaver skins and 2 bear skins, but Falling Rock had not yet returned. After another several weeks, no one had heard or seen from Falling Rock. Even today, one can see along many highways "WATCH OUT FOR FALLING ROCK"*

80

Behind the Winkler house in Troy, there was a giant water-tower. Before approaching the city, I would tell the kids not to be afraid of the looming 'Green Monster' ahead.

Papa Lou died on May 7, 1977 of heart failure, in Troy, NY, at age 74. They had four great children, *Caryl Irene*, *Phyllis Adrian* (died June 28, 2011), *Morris Harry* (died August 11, 2011), and of course Sandy.

Sandy's favorite jewelry was her father's diamond ring. When he died, it was given to his son *Morris*, when he passed, he bequeathed it to Sandy. However, *Marilynn* refused to give it to her, instead she sent it to his daughter *Stephanie* (died November 12, 2012). When she passed, her mother *Leslie* (Morris' first wife), removed the ring off her finger, sent it to Sandy; who has cherished and worn it daily.

Betty: Sandy's mother, *Elizabeth 'Bessie' Mae Levin* was born in Bennington, VT, on May 20, 1906. After Lou died, she took turns visiting each of her kids: Phyllis, Caryl, Morris, and us. At one point, while she was visiting us in Connecticut, she had had a heart attack, but survived. After her recovery, she spent a few days at our home. On one night Sandy cooked dinner and invited her cardiologist and our Rabbi *Mike Manson*. What better company could Nana Betty have had?

All their kids and families came frequently to Troy to visit with Nana Betty and Papa Lou; the house was always full of company. The pantry and credenza was always filled with candy, chocolates and pistachio nuts.

She loved to knit, making sweaters for everyone, not only her grandkids but everyone she met. She died peacefully in her home, with all her children present, on November 19, 1978 of heart failure (and a broken heart), in Troy, NY, at age 72.

Part 3:

The Sixty's

(1960 - 1969)

◇◇◇◇◇◇◇◇◇◇◇◇◇◇◇◇◇◇◇◇

My Career

After graduation, I was given a position as Design Engineer in the Avionics department at *Sikorsky Aircraft* (June 1960- May 1962) in Stratford, CT. Here I designed navigation equipment for helicopters. I had a total of seven offers, but Sikorsky's seemed the best, started at an annual salary of $7,800- **WOW**. Sandy and I lived in an apartment in Bridgeport, only a short ride to work. But, I hated working at Sikorsky, so after a short two year stint, I left.

STORY: On one of my Sikorsky projects (consisting of 33 blueprints); my boss signed them, and put them carefully in a lined waste basket. When returning the next day, there were the charred remains of all the drawings I had worked on. What happened to my boss? Nothing, I just had to redo it.

I joined *Sound Scriber Corp* (June 1962- August 1963) in North Haven, as an engineer designing miniature portable tape recorders used by the CIA (could fit into a cigarette pack) and another one that was used by morticians for autopsies. As I wanted to learn more about designing with plastics, I took an evening course in Plastics Design at SPI. It suggested that I join a toy company where I would have more hands-on involvement with plastics.

Following that recommended career path, I joined the *A.C. Gilbert Co.*, on September 1963 in New Haven, as their Engineering Manager. This was a company involved in the design and manufacture of boy's toys. Their saying was *"There's a Gilbert toy for every boy."* I finally designed plastic toys and became supervisor of their Engineering Dept.

When Gilbert decided to drop the **HO** train business to concentrate on the larger **S** gauge, they sold off the museum of trains and toys. This started my hobby with trains.

Our biggest project was the *James Bond* 007 *Auto Race* set, which included six injection-molded, painted tiles which would lock together to create a scenic set. The molds for these tiles were built in Portugal and painted at Gilbert's factory in New Haven (the paint and paint equipment was supplied by my friend *Lou Barle*). As we were about to start production, we had a motor problem. So, I had to fly out to meet with the engineers at *Mabuchi Motors*, in Tokyo Japan.

STORY: Enroute, I stopped in Seattle, and missed my on-going connection. And in doing so I left my passport and boarding pass on board the plane. I had dinner at the Seattle Space Needle that night, then flew the next day from Seattle to Vancouver, then on to Tokyo, where I spent several hours to get cleared (without my docs), before being released.

Next, in January 1967 I joined the *Ideal Toy Co.*, based in Jamaica, NY, where I was hired as their Engineering Manager for Doll Design. As we still lived in Wallingford, I commuted 86 miles each way to the office. Soon thereafter, I was given the opportunity to become the Director of Far East Manufacturing. I became responsible for all the production and quality of their entire imported toy and doll lines. I traveled frequently to Hong Kong, sometimes for 4-6 weeks at a time. Sandy was solely responsible for bringing up our kids, and, at times, my kids barely knew me when I returned. This proved to be a very difficult time for Sandy.

STORY: In May 1987, for my 50th birthday, Sandy bought me a computer, the first time I had ever used one. Helaine (who worked in computers), procured it (complete with printer and necessary software) from 47th *Street Photo*. I tried, and tried, but could not get it to work. Thinking it was broken, I brought the computer back to the store; where they told me that I was missing DOS. In Yiddish, *Dos* means 'that,' and I assumed he was trying to communicate in Yiddish. I kept saying *Dos*, he kept saying DOS...

Sandy

Sandy and I met while I was at RPI, as their USY counselor. We went steady for a while, then broke up (at dinner at the *Copacabana Club* in NYC), then reunited back together again. Sandy went to *Fisher Junior College*, in Boston, MA. I went to see her every 2nd weekend (on alternate weekends I visited my widowed mother in NYC).

STORY: During one of those visits to Sandy's college, my car broke down and I had to proceed by bus. I was broke when I arrived in Boston, so I donated blood for which I got $20, enough to last thru the weekend.

STORY: In another visit to Boston, Sandy and I went to a Chinese restaurant. As I was about to pay I realized that I had left my wallet at her uncle *Harvey's* house. The restaurant held Sandy hostage until I returned with my wallet.

After college, I wanted to join the Peace Corps, but Sandy wanted to get married. So, right after my graduation, we did get hitched, on June 25, 1960, at Beth El Synagogue, in Troy, NY.

Helaine

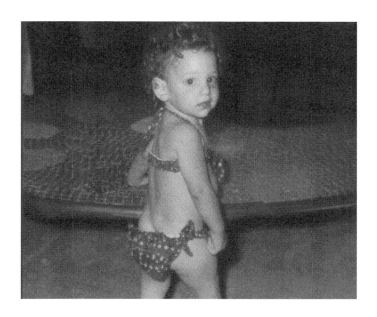

Helaine *Sue,* our first, was born on April 20, 1962 at *St. Vincent's* Hospital, Bridgeport. I prepared the following birth announcement:

Chief Engineer:	**BERT**	Sex:	**GIRL**
Production Mgr:	**SANDY**	Weight:	**8lb 4oz**
Technician:	**DR HOROWITZ**	Eyes:	**BLUE**
Mfg Facility:	**ST. VINCENT**	Hair:	**NONE**
Date:	**APRIL 20, 1962**	Lungs:	**LOUD**

STORY: After arriving at the hospital where Sandy gave birth, I was quite flustered and anxious, and did not see the "OUT OF ORDER" sign posted conspicuously on the elevator doors. I got stuck when the doors closed. The nun, who helped me out by forcing the doors open, scolded me for not reading the sign! Not sure if Sandy believed me?

When she was little, because of her long legs, I used to address her as 'Spider Monkey.'

87

STORY: When Helaine was only a few months old, on Sundays, I would relieve Mom and take care of changing and feeding Helaine. On one such occasion, I tied her down onto the dressing-table, but neglected to put the belt around her. As I was in the bathroom disposing the diaper, I heard a loud cry, to find she had fallen off the 4' high table. Fortunately, she was ok.

STORY: Helaine and I both loved animals. As she grew up, we frequented the Beardsley Park Zoo. One day we visited a neighborhood pet shop that had a very cute Spider monkey. I told her to ignore the sign which stated "DO NOT FEED THE MONKEY". Helaine, following my advice did so, and when she stopped feeding him, the monkey peed on her.

When she was 5 years old, she contracted Typhoid Fever caught from her grandmother Omi, (she was a carrier but had never had the disease herself). I was in Hong Kong, when I got the call that she was in the hospital, and to immediately take the next flight home. This was a very traumatic experience for us all. She had an extremely high temperature, that would not go down. At first the doctors at Yale had no idea what was causing it. Fortunately, with the proper medication, Helaine survived and grew up to become a beautiful and accomplished woman.

Growing up, we lived in a split-level home in *Wallingford*, where Helaine (being taller) would stand behind me brushing her hair in our only bathroom. Helaine was very active and accomplished in high school, excelling in every endeavor. She joined several clubs, the Key-club, the swim-team (butterfly), became a cheerleader, worked as a waitress, as an aide at *Brook Hollow Nursing* home, and then as a Marketing intern at Coleco, where I worked. When she started driving, although she was an excellent and careful driver, we were always worried about a potential car-accident (but we never worried about drugs, pregnancy, etc).

88

Helaine's best friends growing up were *Ann Nastri*, *Jackie Doyle* and *Joey Sayers*. She often babysat for the *Canny*, *Rosoff*, and *Goldstein* kids. Helaine and I spent a lot of time together as she grew up. We often cheered her on at her swim-meets. As a teenager, Helaine was difficult, and did not get along with her mother, who, when she was 12, threw her out of the house. Helaine slept that night in the woods!

STORY: When she was not swimming, I would take her to *Drazen Lumber* in North Haven, where I would have her count screws and nuts. I later found out that she hated going there, **I wonder why**?.

STORY: When Helaine was about seven, she ran to catch her school bus and was hit by a moving car. (They didn't have the automatic STOP signs on school buses we have today). She got a concussion and was rushed to the hospital where she threw up her breakfast (salami). As a result of this accident, she never ate salami again.

STORY: Most of the family loved to ski, but Helaine did not. On a rare day when she and I went up the slope, I (mistakenly) took her up the EXPERT slope. She never skied with me again.

STORY: While at the Peabody Museum, I slapped Helaine for being disobedient in front of some of her friends. She was very embarrassed; I never hit her again. Being the oldest, she had a lot of responsibility, occasionally taking care of her two younger brothers, cleaning the kitchen, mowing the lawn, babysitting, while still getting A's.

During Helaine's high school, I lectured about my years in the Shanghai Ghetto to *George Doyle*'s history class (I did that in Eric and Dana's classes as well). The instructor pointed out that it was in his class that Helaine and Harold had first met and later married!

STORY: In 1986, the whole family made a trip to Hong Kong. On the day before Christmas, we toured the *Man Mo Temple* on Hong Kong Island; then on to the *Landmark Shopping Mall*; then on to our tailor in *Tsim Sha Tsui*, Kowloon for a fitting. Somewhere between the Hong KongIsland and the Kowloon mainland, Helaine, Harold, and Eric got separated from the rest of us; Sandy was sure that they had been kidnapped! She was hysterical wanting me to call the Police and the American Embassy! After a grueling several hours, they finally showed, having stopped at McDonald's.

Helaine graduated with honors from the *University of Massachusetts* at Amherst, MA with a degree in Communications. While in college, she also worked at *Cumberland Farms*, *Lenny's* Café, *Jonathan Jay's* Restaurant, and at *Bobby Rosoff's Durham Inn* and Restaurant.

Sandy and I were concerned about the forthcoming 'mixed' marriage of Helaine (Jewish) and Harold (Catholic). Sandy approached Bill and Ann and asked about their thoughts. They too had spoken with their priest, querying about the proposed inter-marriage; to which he replied *"No one knows who is right?"*

Helaine and Harold were married on September 1, 1985 at *Aqua-Turf Club*, in Southington. Officiating was Rabbi *Davidson*, and later (at the following party) were Rabbi *Manson* and Father *O'Neil* who blessed the couple. At the head-table were a Cabbage Patch bride and groom, made for them by one of my Cabbage Patch subcontractors.

STORY: In my excitement, the day before the wedding, I accidently backed my car without looking, nearly maiming the bride.

In 1996, Helaine and I created a toy marketing company: '*Momentum Marketing*', a division of REINER Associates. We developed ideas and represented some toy inventors, then tried selling them to toy manufacturers in return for royalty. Some examples were:

Kiddy Keyboard- Keyboard Overlay (presented to Hasbro)"
"The emerging pre-school PC computer software market has been virtually untapped, either the current keyboard layout is not age appropriate, or an additional pre-school keyboard is extremely costly. An opportunity exists to become the market share leader of this category by introducing a sophisticated, yet simple to use, low cost product bundled with your software. The "Kiddy Keyboard" is an inviting keyboard overlay which fits over any standard 101 key PC keyboard; which encourages pre-school children to play or learn, with software specifically developed for their age group. The "Kiddy Keyboard" provides a simple overlay with large, decorated keys to fit over the standard PC keyboard, enabling the child to focus on the myriad of possible software products for his/her age group".

Now You're Talking-Motion-activation (presented to Pepsi):
"Now You're Talking" is a self-contained, motion-activated voice module. The unit plays a variety of pre-recorded announcements to direct attention toward a Pepsi vending machine — as someone passes in front of the motion detector, the recording plays. The motion-activated voice chip can be pre-recorded with a series of messages or announcements and can play randomly, sequentially, or timed at pre-set intervals. The unit is designed to be compact enough to fit easily inside a vending machine or electronic kiosk, without any retrofit".

Eric

Eric *Howard* came next, our 'middle' son; born on March 4, 1966 at *World War II Memorial* Hospital, in Meriden. When he was only 3 months old, Eric suffocated while we had left him alone in a car-bed (under supervision of *Leibschen*) in the parking lot of *Arthur's*, in Hamden. Thankfully, we arrived in time; to see he had turned blue, with mouth-to-mouth resuscitation I brought him back to life.

STORY: In August 1978, I had taken a trip with Eric to tour the *Smithsonian Institute* in Washington, DC. It was a great experience, however, when we left, my (rented) car was towed because I had it illegally parked. After several taxi trips to find the Auto Impound Lot, we found out that the car was merely towed onto the sidewalk, and never left the area.

STORY: We had celebrated Eric's 6th birthday with several of his friends at Burger King. When it was time to go, my mother helped to round up the kids, but one was reluctant to go, he cried refusing to budge. It turns out, he was not part of our group and my mother almost kidnapped him.

STORY: While I had emptied (for maintenance) our above-ground swimming pool, Eric and his sister jumped into the deep-end hopper, sustaining a 4 foot long gash in the liner. That was not the only damage this 'duo team' had done; they broke a Coleco prototype big-wheel; and also my watch (after putting it in the washing-machine).

STORY: Eric got hurt quite often. On March 2, 1976, at age 10, Eric broke his leg while skiing and had to wear a cast. At another time, he got his tongue stuck on the refrigerator's ice-maker (required stitches). While at YMCA camp one summer, he fell asleep on the bus enroute home. His friend *Adam Herzlich* never woke him up when the bus stopped; the bus continued and finally dropped Eric off at the Cheshire Police Department.

Eric was frequently late catching his bus going to high school, so I would have to drive him to get him there on time. He rarely studied, yet always got very high marks. While in high school, Eric had a newspaper route, worked at *Ye Old Ice Cream* shop, was a waiter at *Chao's Garden Chinese* restaurant, waiter at the *Wallingford Country Club*, Model Maker at Coleco (who got him that job?), and worked with Harold to paint houses. While in high school, Eric's best friend was *Matt Poach*.

Growing up, Eric was a big help to me: He helped lay patio-blocks, and weed between the blocks (because I forgot to lay black PE film underneath); built a huge wooden porch; built my Japanese 'relaxation' garden; paneled and installed ceiling beams in the basement; converted my garage to a den with a sunken fireplace pit; and many more.

STORY: One Summer, I got Eric an interesting job; he and Matt traveled throughout the U.S. repairing *Verbot* and *Omnibot* robots at (18) Toys-R-Us warehouses. Although well paid, I was frequently called when he ran out of money.

STORY: On one Rosh Hashanah Eric got a *'Hagbah Aliya'* (to raise the Torah), to which he said *"Jesus, this is heavy"*, to which Rabbi *Manson* replied *"wrong place"*.

STORY: As I was still struggling with starting my own consulting firm, Eric's wedding would soon become a big expense. *'Whom to invite and whom not to?'* became an ongoing discussion between Sandy and myself. I had a solution... ask all our friends, neighbors and relatives for a $5,000 loan, whomever agreed, would be invited! But, we elected not to do that.

Eric went on to *Rensselaer Polytechnic Institute* (RPI) [my alma-mater], earning both Baccalaureate (1989) and Masters (1992) degrees in Bio-Medical Engineering. After a short stint as an EMT and then at *U.S. Surgical*, Eric got his DO doctorate at the *University of New England College of Osteopathic Medicine* (on June 7, 1997). After completing his residences at *St. Raphael*, *Albany Medical*, and *Yale*, Eric became a Board Certified *Interventional Radiologist*.

Eric and Gail were married July 2, 1994 at *High Lane Tennis Club.* in North Haven, CT. True to form of always being late at their wedding whilst the music had already started, Eric was still stapling flowers onto the *'Chupah'* (marriage canopy).

QUOTE: **"In the end, it's not the years in your life that counts, it's the life in your years"**
Abraham Lincoln

94

Dana

Dana; Next came our youngest son *Dana Owen*, born on June 12, 1971 at *Yale New Haven Hospital*. Bright and enthusiastic, he was clearly to become the 'salesman' of the family. When he was born, his mother's OBGYN *Dr. Krosnick* urged me to witness his birth and to cut his umbilical, but I could not—Instead I watched TV in the waiting room. I was satisfied with having only two kids - Sandy wanted three; I'm so glad that Sandy persisted!

During Dana's infant years, he frequently had croup, solved by putting him in the shower. He was always mischievous (I wonder where he got that from?). He was often seen in his high-chair with a handful of Cheerios, with a grape-tomato on his nose.

STORY: When he was about five, he and his best-friend *David Canny* rough-housed on our lawn, killing my seven year old Japanese Maple. While at *Beardsley Park* petting-zoo, Dana was feeding a deer and was thrown by another (jealous) deer into the air, with his antlers.

95

STORY: While at a picnic at our neighbor *Jack Doyle's*, he warned Dana to be careful that the BBQ grill was hot. Dana was arguing with Jack that the grill could not be hot because it was not red. To prove his point, Dana stepped on the grill, whereupon Jack threw him in the pool to cool of.

STORY: Each summer, the boys, Eric, Dana and/or *Rick Canny, David Canny*, *Justin Barle* and I, traveled on a camping trip to Vermont or New Hampshire. Of course, I did the cooking. My specialty being clams and linguini; which I always managed to spill onto the fire.

STORY: Once, while dinning at *Wo Hop*, our favorite Chinatown restaurant, Dana (on a $5 dare) reached over to a nearby table, picked up and ate their fried noodle.

Dana always loved the Arcades, also 'Dungeons and Dragons', playing games for several hours at a time. When he was too little to really play, we would go to restaurants with video arcades, so he could 'play' the demo games (but without inserting any quarters).

STORY: While at Bradley Airport, we noticed *Henry Winkler* (star of *Happy Days*) at Arrivals waiting for his luggage. Dana approached him and said that his grandfather was a 'Winkler', too. Henry Winkler replied *"who cares, leave me alone kid"*, which left Dana very disillusioned.

STORY: When Dana was young, he traveled with us to Hong Kong, when I told him how to negotiate when we got there. Soon after we arrived, we saw a Chinese clerk following Dana, trying to persuade him to buy a cloisonné vase. What was a 12 year old going to do with a vase? He merely learning and practicing how to 'bargain'.

While in high school, Dana belonged to several clubs and jobs: SADD and Key Club; worked at *All Pets Supplies*;

at *Vinny Garden Center*; at digging ponds; and helped Harold with painting houses (but wasn't very good at it). He also excelled in skiing, which led him to be a ski-instructor at *Mount Southington* Ski Resort.

STORY: Each year we would travel to Buffalo to celebrate Passover with *Caryl* and *Marvin*. Enroute on one of those trips, we stopped at a rest-stop, and I accidently left Dana behind. After several miles, I asked Eric why Dana was so quiet, he then replied that Dana was left behind but he was told to be quiet, and not to say a word.

At 6, the following was Dana's complaints about Eric:

1. *Thros a cher at me.*   7. *Hrts hulane.*
2. *Punches me.*   8. *Wont let me yos mikwuwave*
3. *Yels at me.*   9. *Thros my elbo in a cher.*
4. *Sckreems at hulane.*   10. *Bracks miey pnsel.*
5. *Teses me.*   11. *Fitse hulane.*
6. *Lise on me.*   12. *Yels at the dogs.*

STORY: On June 2, 1984, Dana had his Bar Mitzvah at *Pilgrim Harbor Golf Course (*where we owned our second home). At each table was a *Cabbage Patch Kid*, one mother (not a good friend) stole one off a child's table. All the kids made an uproar, so she reluctantly returned it. In 1988 Dana got an 'Outstanding Academic Achievement' award signed by president George W. Bush (not sure for what)?

The following was Dana's Bar Mitzvah speech:

"As I stand here today, with humility and some nervousness, I pledge to fulfill my responsibilities and obligations as a Jew. I received tonight, and am wearing for the first time, my *Talit*. It has special meaning to me, as it had belonged to my grandfather Papa Lou. This is a very important religious symbol worn by all Jewish men during their daily prayers. It is

interesting to note that the numerical value of the letters of the word *Tzizit* (the fringes) is six hundred, and together with the eight long threads and the five knots, total 613; which happens to be the number of righteous acts contained within the *Torah*. My Papa Lou was such a devout person, he most probably did most of these *Mitzvot*.

Since a *Talit* is not to be kept unused, I feel honored to receive and wear his. In the years to come, I will pledge to follow in his footsteps, to lead a life of honesty, charity and integrity, and to help make this world a better place to live. I feel fortunate to have had the proper foundation to start me on my way; my parents, grandparents, rabbi, teachers, to you all I am grateful.

As my father, and my ancestors before me, I too have taken on an obligation to be be worthy as a *Kohen*. Aaron was the first Kohen (high priest) during the Exodus from Egypt.

To my friends and family, my thanks to you all for wanting to share this moment with me. My parents and I wish to invite you to the *Oneg Shabat*, which will be held at our home.

Like his sister, Dana went to *UMass*, in Amherst MA, graduating with a Bachelor degree in Business Administration, with a minor in Finance. While in college, he belonged to *Sigma Alpha Mu* fraternity. He often helped me with doing odd-jobs, such as painting ski figures for the *Santa's Ski Slope* (one of REINER work projects).

Dana and Angela were married on June 13, 1998 at the *Glen Island Harbor Club*, in New Rochelle, NY. They had two weddings, first at *Our Lady Of Pity Roman Catholic Church*, followed by the Jewish Ceremony at the *Glen Island Club*. As it was customary to sign the '*Ketubah*' (marriage license) before the ceremony, we found out that the 'rabbi' could not read Hebrew! Was he really an ordained rabbi? Are Dana and Angela really married?

Marriage Encounter

Although *Marriage Encounter* was originally formed for couples in the Catholic faith (started by *Father Calvo* in Spain); there now exist many Jewish Marriage Encounter groups that can be found throughout the world. The one we attended was sponsored by *Temple Beth Sholom* in Hamden. Having been married for only a few years we decided to try the idea of "making a good marriage even better". This two day retreat was held at a Spa in Western Connecticut, far from home. We were a little nervous not knowing what to expect. After checking in, we began to get a taste of the beautiful and inspiring weekend that was about to begin. The encounter was facilitated by the rabbi and his wife.

We had choices of several workshops and topics. Some we did together, some separately. We were given notebooks for expressing our thoughts and then read to each other after each session. For the separate sessions on intimacy we parted ways and then compared our notes afterward.

We learned how to better communicate with each other, leaving us feeling even closer than we did before. We met people of all ages, some married only a few months, some over 20 years. Listening to all the potential and actual problems arise during marriage was a real eye-opener for us and gave us new appreciation for our own marriage.

We later encouraged many of our friends to attend such an encounter. It was a great and fulfilling weekend.

QUOTE: **"If it's worth doing, then do it well".**
Horace Reiner.

Mira-Plate

One evening, our friend *Lou Barle* was telling us about a business he was starting he called *Mira-Plate*. It looked very promising, and I wanted in! When one purchases perfume, the bottle is usually comes covered with a gold cap, which is usually done by a process called 'vacuum-metalizing'; The colorless caps are installed on a rack, placed in a vacuum chamber, and aluminum vaporized and deposited with a fine film of 'silver color', then coated with a yellow die to give it the 'gold' color. Lou, however, was supplying lacquers to a company that had a unique process which involved only spraying a microscopic coat of real silver directly onto the caps; this proved to be considerably less costly process.

It sounded like a great idea, so I invested $7,000 for a 14% interest in the company (this investment eventually became $17,000). Our neighbor, *Jack Doyle* also invested, as did my brother-in-law Marvin (for printing) and Sandy's dad (for corrugated cartons). The person we hired was Mike, whom we thought to be the expert. Alas, he knew <u>nothing</u> about the chemistry needed to facilitate to process. I was responsible for researching, selecting, and buying the equipment, conveyors, spray booths, etc. Sandy was responsible for hiring and training the work-force, and Lou for the sales; everything worked at par, except for Mike's part. He had no idea what to do, and the business failed.

We had an SBA loan which we faulted, so we lost a total of $97,000 in the 9 months we were in operation. The lesson I learned was **"stick to what I know"**!

GR+R

Together with our close friends *Nate Goldstein*, and *Bobby Rosoff*, we formed a real-estate company called **GR+R**; which proved not to be very successful; it was actually a disaster! We first invested in a 3-family, 3-story house in East Haven, which was difficult to maintain, and no money.

STORY: In this house, we had some tenants (two single women) who were not paying their rent. We finally hired a locksmith to change their lock and put a sign on the door for them to call us if/when they returned. When they indeed came back, they called the police, and claimed that we stole sound equipment worth $200, (the precise amount that they owed us). Nate and I went promptly to the house and met with the police, who presented us with an arrest warrant. The police believed us, but we needed to hire a lawyer to settle.

STORY: We next owned a Laundromat in East Haven. While I was doing some repairs to a large washing machine, three year-old Eric opened the door while in full-operation; he got swept across the floor to the other end of the Laundromat. We even lost money in the change-machine.

Then we upgraded to a 5-family house, in Meriden; which was an even bigger loser. We took turns collecting rents and making repairs. Sometimes, when I was too busy, Sandy went out to collect rents, she often returned without money, but had bought milk for their kids because their fridge was empty. On one occasion I was even threatened with a switch-blade knife when I pulled out her fuses.

When we finally sold it (was still on 'pending sale'), we saw on television that the house was on fire. The sale obviously fell through and we lost everything. That ended my career as a real estate magnum. Again, the lesson I learned was "**stick to what I know**"!

101

Part 4:

The Coleco Years

(1969 - 1988)

◇◇◇◇◇◇◇◇◇◇◇◇◇◇◇◇

The Job

On April 14, 1969 I joined *Coleco Industries* in Hartford, CT as their Engineering Manager. Later on, Coleco was at that time the 3rd largest toy company in the U.S. It was started by *Leonard Greenberg* (died July 12, 2017) and *Mel Gershman* (died September 4, 2013), in his father *Maurice Greenberg's* shop, making leather kits; **COLECO** is an anagram for [COnnecticut LEather COmpany].

Maurice was an immigrant from Ukraine who came to the U.S. in 1911. He started working in New Haven, until he moved to Hartford. When Wall Street crashed in 1929, the start of the Great Depression, it was the worst economic crisis the world had ever seen. However, shortly thereafter, on February 29, 1932, he opened the doors to the Connecticut

Leather Company, as a distributor to shoemakers with leather and shoe findings. His son Leonard, at only 16, started making and selling hand-crafted leather items. After college, he started to produce handbags, wallets, moccasins. billfolds, key cases, and make-yourself leather-craft kits. From there, they later expanded to making vacuum-formed pools, sleds and toboggans. Coleco purchased *Kestral* which was then making steel-walled, vinyl-lined swimming pools.

STORY: Maurice was extremely frugal, one day, while in the Asylum avenue facility, I was in the bathroom when he criticized me for having used TWO paper towels to wash my hands, he said *"wouldn't just one have been sufficient?"*

As Coleco's Engineering Manager, I was responsible for the design of swimming pools (from 10' diameter to 32' oval) and accessories (ladders, skimmers, filters, etc). Eventually, on January 1975 I was promoted to VP of Product Development, and in February 1985 I became Senior Vice President of Quality Assurance. On May 13 1988, after 19 years with Coleco, I was laid off, and the following month they declared bankruptcy.

STORY: Leonard's son *Robert Greenberg*, was one of the first twelve programmers at Microsoft. His father had lent them money, and when Bob left, he was offered to have the loan returned, or given Microsoft stock. He chose the former.

STORY: In 1962, the *Bowl-A-Matic* was one of the games we manufactured. As a result of a complaint which was received by *Arnold Greenberg,* he wrote to me: "If this woman is right that our instruction sheet states '...*This is the part of the stringing of the game for the woman in your family'*, then we are really big sexist schmucks. We've got no business saying anything as stupid as this in this day and age". P.S. The wording came from his brother Leonard.

104

It was said that Coleco was run like a Jewish delicatessen; "whoever screamed the loudest, got what they wanted". I always had to fight for my promotions; the following is a letter I wrote to Arnold on May 8, 1984; (prior to my promotion to Sr. VP):

"**Coleco now has two Product Development groups: One (Computer) has had serious difficulties, whereas the other (Toys) is running smoothly. My point can best be expressed with the following analogy: A family has two children, one child has a drug problem, whilst the other is a studious, conscientious individual. All the attention is given to the troubled one, the other goes unnoticed. It therefore seems necessary for me to bring to your attention some of my recent accomplishments:**

1. Although we will soon have a total of five Cabbage Patch doll manufacturers, I had introduced both Kader and Perfekta, whose total production will be supplying 85% of shipments.

2. We have all taken for granted, but few are aware, of the complexity to manufacture Cabbage Patch. The concept of producing an infinite variety of <u>different </u>dolls, but still be mass producible, is a unique concept. Contrary to our own PR, they are not differentiated by computer, but by a complicated matrix which I had developed. No other toy company has ever attempted to produce such a toy concept.

3. During my recent Orient trip, I was asked to stay an additional week to maximize the shipments for the 1st quarter. Results: the second highest sales quarter in Coleco history! That last little push, urging the vendors to work until 2:00am, may have made the difference. This also included my offering Perfekta a $0.25 bonus above their 8K/day rate (despite Leonard's objections). Result: additional 110K dolls in March.

4. A week before Christmas, I was in Washington at CPSC to avert a disaster with Pizza-Oven by preventing a product recall.

105

5. Our finances are tight right now, Paul asked that I request D/A terms from Kader; I negotiated a $3 million open credit line. Also I negotiated extended terms with Kam Toys; 60 day terms with an agreement for us to pay our existing $750K debt over the next eight weeks.

6. During the development of this year's toy lines, there was less involvement by Management than ever before. Under my direction, working closely with Marketing, the gross profit of the Toy and Doll division are the highest ever.

7. I am also responsible for the Engineering Support Groups. All the drafting gets done; sales models are available for Toy Fair and CES; all instruction sheets get done for ColecoVision and Adam (no matter how late the release of software). All this done in spite of frequent trips to the Orient.

8. The Outdoor line is running smoothly without problems: The CPK Clubhouse was scheduled to start 2/1, the first shipment was made on February 6th. The Ride-On line has already commenced with all items (except Knight-Rider car), the earliest ever! All Cabbage Patch accessories will be in production by June. This is being achieved by (14) Orient trips already taken by myself and members of my staff.

Unfortunately, my pride has suffered in having to recount some of these accomplishments to you. But, you will be provided with the peace of mind to know that the job will get done. I would have much preferred not to have had to bring this pen to paper; hopefully my position will now be respected and recognized.   Sincerely, *Bert*

On almost all Saturdays you would find me working at Coleco, while our kids were eating junk-food; Helaine was at my secretary's typewriter. (My secretary *Linda* hated when she arrived on Mondays to find the keys all sticky); Eric and Dana played with video arcade games (no quarters needed);

106

and Sandy telephoning Aunt Caryl for FREE. Frequently I brought toys and games for my kids and friends to play with and frequently to check out the instructions. I was known as the '**favorite father on the block**'!

Ike Pearlmutter, owner of *Odd Lots,* had a lot of cash. He, together with *Mort Handel* (CFO), persuaded Coleco to sell their excess inventory to Ike in exchange for TV time through Admerex [ADvertising MERchandise EXchange]. That proved to be a sham as the TV showings were valueless, given the late night showings, long after the kids were asleep.

I amassed several grants, totaling 4,000 shares of Coleco stock. During the 1984 CES, Coleco announced and presented the Adam Computer which was a huge success. The stock jumped to $84/share. As I was an officer of the company, I had to follow SEC Rule 144 to sell any stock. I decided to sell only 1,000 shares (25% of my holdings), as Arnold had said for me to hold, because the stock would keep going up. I filled out the necessary forms, got corporate approval, registered with the NYSE, and advised my broker that I would be ready to sell. At 9:00am the following Monday I got a call from my broker, but my secretary intercepted the call and advised him that I was in a staff meeting. When I returned his call three hours later, the stock had dropped to $78/share. I decided to sell only 200 shares. What a mistake! After that, the stock kept declining, until I finally sold the balance at $3.50/share. When Coleco sold off it's holdings when it filed chapter 11 bankruptcy, the remaining assets became 'Ranger Corp' headed by *MortHandel* and *Mike Schwefel,* who swindled most of what money was left.

Swimming Pool Years 1969-75

I was hired by *Mel Gershman* as Coleco's first engineer and becoming their Engineering Manager. I joined this company against my will, as Sandy was unwilling for us to relocate to Newark, NJ where I had gotten a job offer from *Remco*. But, designing 10 to 32 foot swimming pools was not appealing to me. I traveled to the Upstate factories (Gloversville, Amsterdam and Mayfield, NY) for several days each week; at night I stayed at the Johnstown Holiday Inn. I generally traveled Upstate with Mel. He was the worst boss I ever had; he believed in management by intimidation!

STORY: I had hired *Ed Greenberg*, (Mel's brother-in-law) as my Engineering Manager. After a few months, I found that he was not capable of managing this position, and I was about to fire him. As a courtesy to Mel, I told him of my plans; he told me that I was an incapable manager, then told Ed (his wife's brother): "*to get a broom and sweep the floors, because Bert said that's all you're capable of.*"

Fortunately, I was given the task of designing and manufacturing a line of swimming pool Filters to be sold with the pools, which I found very challenging. This was done in conjunction with the engineers at *Eagle Toys*, in Montreal.

108

They were then making Vibrator football, hockey games, and the *Alouette* snowmobiles. So, for the next two years, I traveled each week (away from Mel), from Monday to Thursday to our Montreal plant. At night I would stay at the Ruby Foo motel.

STORY: When the toy company *Remco* filed for bankruptcy (I had almost worked for them), I attended their auction selling off factory equipment and toy molds. I purchased (on Coleco's behalf), lots of 'stuff', i.e. (40) power screwdrivers, (2) injection molding machines, (6) power presses, several molds for a game, and a silo to hold 180,000# plastic resin. Mel blasted me for buying the latter: *"You had no authority to buy such equipment, we had no space for something so large, and we did not need it"*. A year later the country was in a severe plastic resin shortage, the silo was greatly needed; I then became a **hero**.

Several patents were awarded to me for swimming pool pumps (#3,644,760), drains (#3,685,657), and filters (#3,767,050). I became a member of the NSPI Safety committee, and was instrumental in developing Safety Standards for Above-ground pools, ladders and filters.

At 8:30am each morning, we had our FAX meeting in the conference room. All key Operations' personnel were in attendance, reviewing the news of the day; Leonard usually chaired the meeting. We would read that day's faxes from Asia, and each of us would discuss what action needed to be taken.

On January 1, 1975, I was promoted to VP of Product Development. I became responsible for Coleco's Engineering, Instruction group, Model Shop, PCB departments. Unfortunately, I was still continuing to report to Mel.

Telstar Years 1976-78

Following the craze of *Odyssey* (Magnavox) and *Pong* (Atari), Coleco embarked into the video game industry and introduced 'Telstar'. In 1976, I contracted *Alpex Engineering Co.*, in Danbury, CT, to develop a more featured video game. But, they found that *General Instrument* (GI) had a chip already under development in their Scotland facilities which was vastly superior, and would soon become available. I persuaded Arnold to placed an order with GI for those chips at $5.00 each, who then gave Coleco a six month exclusivity. We sold 950,000 video games that year! Unfortunately, as soon as the exclusive period ran out, GI flooded the market. At the following CES show there were 28 companies selling the same game.

Before we could start production, we needed to get FCC approval. I packed up the unit and went off to Washington DC, but the game flunked. I immediately contracted *Bill Slovak* of *Novatech* in Chicago, to help solve the RFI problem. He came with a basket of goodies, a small ferrite coil solved it, and we got the FCC certification.

110

It was obvious that we needed to go overseas for our electronic production, and we also needed an agent. As I had known *Al Simmons* from my previous jobs, I negotiated a contract with his company *Tri-State* to become our agents. I then arranged to have *Alan Cheng* (whose cousin worked for Al), for me to visit (18) factories in Hong Kong and Taiwan; of those, I selected *Zeny*, located in Kaohsiung, Taiwan.

STORY: The following year, Coleco came out with the *Telstar Ranger*, where you would shoot with a pistol at targets on the TV screen. While carrying several of those pistol samples from Mainland China through Taiwan Customs, I was approached by several soldiers who almost arrested me because these guns looked so real.

In the early years, traveling to and from China was very difficult. Entering China, we had to declare calculators, watches, cameras, and any jewelry that we were carrying. When we left China, Customs would compare what you had, with what you entered with. If anything was missing (presumed left in China), one would have to pay a stiff fine.

In 1977 Coleco contracted with the *Marvin Glass* Co., of Chicago, IL well known toy creators and innovators, (who had designed some of the most successful toys and games of this century) to design a toy optical-electronic shooting gallery, the *'Shoot'N'Score'*.

STORY: While in the Marvin Glass offices one morning, their project designer went berserk and killed their president *Anson Isaacson* and two other employees, wounded several others, then killed himself. It was scary to realize that he had sat directly behind me in my car the day before.

In 1978, Coleco's R+D department (headed by *Eric Bromley* whom I had hired), developed the *'Electronic Quarterback Football'*. Although a 'knock-off' of Mattel's, the game and display were vastly superior. *Mark Yoseloff* (whom I had also hired) introduced the notable difference, that we had two blockers giving the quarterback the ability to pass. Most famous was their marketing strategy, showing a TV commercial with two guys showing off the Coleco vs. the

Mattel game. The commercial was unique and paid off. My department had grown to 95 persons and the Advanced Development was broken off to become the *ARD Group*.

STORY: During one of my trips to China, I was invited to attend the opening ceremony of a new factory in *Guangzhou* (formerly Canton). I was sitting outdoors, in front of a roasted pig (later to be eaten). During the speeches, while the sun was beating down onto the pig with the fat dripping off, I became nauseous thinking about later eating the skin, basking in the sun.

STORY: Every October or November I would be invited to *Kader Industries* (the largest toy manufacturer in Hong Kong), where we were served fresh-water 'Shanghai (hairy) crabs'; I loved them, eating 10+ per sitting.

I made many, trips to Hong Kong & China, mostly via Pan Am business class. I therefore accumulated lots of World Pass flyer points (Pan Am invented the frequent-flyer concept). When United took over the Pan Am routes, I became a Million Miler; becoming a Gold Premier member for life! While in Hong Kong, I usually stayed at the Royal Garden Hotel, in a Jr. suite.

A very disruptive time of year was the Chinese New Year, when all production comes to a HALT for 4-6 weeks. It must be understood that the employees (mostly girls) come south from the north of China, where travel to their homes could take a week there and another week to return. These young girls (ages 13-19) live on farms, and when they arrive home with a satchel of money they had earned, and now become 'wealthy' and very attractive to the guys. It's not unusual for them to get married, and not return back to work.

Head to Head Years 1979-82

In 1979, Coleco introduced to the world a small computerized toy called the Quiz Wiz (created by *Mark Yoseloff*) to test the limits of your knowledge. This cutting-edge game was equipped with green and red lights for noting correct and incorrect answers to a book with 1,001 questions. There were 20 such books published, covering subjects like Sports, Trivia, Movies & TV, Rock & Roll, People & Places, Super Heroes, etc.

STORY: I had to scour my friends and experts to help write these books. Sandy and her friend *Camille Canny* wrote three of those books. Later, one day they were at a toy store admiring their accomplishments, when they proudly stated to a customer standing by, that they wrote those books, to which she quizzically replied *"sure you did"*.

I have received several more patents consisting of Air Hockey (#3,954,267), Battery Eliminator (#261,881), Video Joy-stick (#4,439,648), Ride-on toy (#4,516,648), and Doll Motion-sensor (#4,766,275).

114

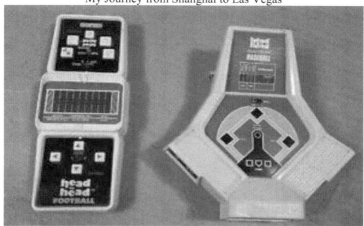

Other hand-held games introduced that year were *Head-to-Head Football, Basketball, Hockey, Galaxian, Alien* and *Zodiac*. The following year, in 1980, Coleco brought into the market the very popular *Head-to-Head Baseball*, and *Star Trek*. We also introduced *Space Blaster, Digits* & *Lil Genius*.

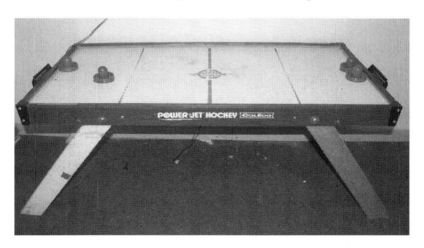

In 1980, Coleco obtained a license from *Brunswick* to produce a line of six foot Air Hockey games. The Upstate factory purchased lots of equipment to route the wood tables, and drill the required 1,200 holes. (*Arnold Greenberg* insisted that we have more holes than our competition).

115

STORY: To produce our sales-models, our model shop bought (20) full-size tables from *Rizzo Pools*, and then cut them down to size. That week, our sales team inquired with Rizzo how their air-hockey table sales were doing. They replied that they were selling like hot-cakes, they had already sold (20) that week. This was also the start of our sports products line, which included pool, ping-pong and basketball.

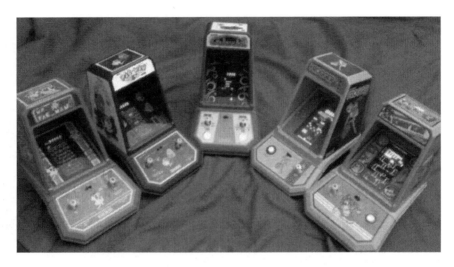

Then in 1981, came one of my favorites, a line of mini-Arcade games; miniature versions of the classic Arcades. Included were *Frogger*, *Donkey Kong*, *DK Jr.*, *Omega Race*, *Zaxxon*, *Galaxian*, *Pac-Man*, and *Ms Pac-Man*. These games were manufactured by *Applied Electronics* (AEL), headed by *Raymond Hung* of Hong Kong.

STORY: My family and I had lunch with Raymond Hung on his boat at the Aberdeen Marina. Looking at our kid's faces, he predicted that Helaine would be a successful entrepreneur, and have 3 children, Harold would give up his opera career, and Eric's 1st girlfriend would cheat on him and he would marry his 2nd girlfriend; all three predictions came true!

116

ColecoVision Years (1982-84)

Coleco's flagship and ultimate achievement in the video game business was *'ColecoVision'*. In 1982, Coleco (via *Eric Bromley, Mark Yoseloff* and the ARD team) introduced a video-game console (using the Zilog Z80 CPU) that offered a closer experience to a more powerful arcade game system compared to the *VCS 2600* (Atari) or the *Intellivision* (Mattel). Included with the console was a *Nintendo Donkey Kong* cartridge. As the prices of RAM chips and display parts were dropping, that's what was needed as they allowed near Arcade resolution. Soon thereafter, additional licenses were signed for *Zaxxon*, *Turbo*, *Lady Bug*, *Cosmic Adventure*, *Smurf*, etc. Over two million consoles were sold that year, with a total of 170 cartridge titles to become available.

Soon after we started to ship the Atari compatible Donkey Kong cartridges, we got complaints that it did not work with 30% of the Atari 2600 consoles. *Mark Yoseloff* assembled his team and found out that Atari had altered their game, (probably to screw Coleco). By adding a capacitor, the problem was solved, 100K cartridges were shipped that year.

117

My Chinese vendors were hungry to get Coleco's business. When I met with *Vincent Li* of *Keysbond*, he offered me Coke, I refused and informed him that I only drank club-soda (not available in China at that time). On our next trip to visit his factory, he had his staff carry a 6-pack. On another trip to visit a prospective vendor in Taipei, I complained about the heat in their conference room. On my next trip to their factory, they had an air-conditioner installed.

STORY: The ColecoVision was also sold throughout Europe with extreme success. In 1983, I traveled with our CEO *Leonard Greenberg,* to Kyoto, Japan to attempt to sell the ColecoVision to *Nintendo*. We met with their president, *Hiroshi Yamauchi*. Leonard offered to sell the game at 10% below our U.S. wholesale price. Nintendo, however, wanted to buy it at 10% above our manufacturing price, so no deal was reached. As we left, their president said that Nintendo would design their own line of video games, Leonard **LAUGHED**! (Nintendo went on to become the largest company in the video game industry)

I would like to share some pointers in business dealings with the Chinese:

1.Always have plenty of business cards. Don't ask for their card, present them with yours and they will quickly respond.

2.The Chinese are not used to the Western habit of touching, it is new for them to even shake hands. The accepted greeting is a slight bow.

3.Use 'checking with the home-office' as a bargaining tactic. Recognize that the Chinese will concede nothing until at the very end of the negotiations.

4.The Chinese avoid saying 'no'. Taking a slower tact will often avoid a cultural blunder and aide in your favor.

Cabbage Patch Years 1983-88

In February, 1983, Coleco introduced the *Cabbage Patch Kids* at the International Toy Fair in New York. These were originally developed by *Xavier Roberts* in Cleveland, GA., where he was making a larger (24") version at the *Baby Land General Hospital*. The factory consisted of 'doctors and nurses' who hand-stitched and manufactured these kids; all different, ready to be <u>adopted</u> (not purchased). Their licensor tried to sell the franchise to Mattel, Hasbro and Marvin Glass, but none were interested, except for our *Al Kahn*.

The day I arrived at Toy Fair in NYC, I was met with *Harvey Zelman* in the elevator, who told me to leave immediately for China, to place orders for these 'ugly dolls', are you kidding? I was corrected when I was told that they were called 'KIDS', not dolls. He was right; in 1983 alone, we sold 3.3 million, with every kid shipped by air!

I was indeed commanded by *Leonard Greenberg* that day to pack up and depart for Hong Kong to find at least two potential suppliers. I approached *Kader* and *Perfecta,* whom I had known as doll manufacturers when I had worked at Ideal.

Talking to these vendors, they both laughed at the prospect to make each kid **DIFFERENT**? That's impossible to do? That night, while at the *Royal Garden* Hotel, I developed the **MATRIX** that made that possible. Each factory would have (8) different head molds, which we rooted with (8) different hair styles, and (12) different hair colors, and (4) different eye colors; that's already (3,072 variations)! Plus, we also had different hair styles, different outfits, white and black, etc., producing a nearly unlimited mix of kids.

STORY: While still at the New York Toy Fair, I had conducted a meeting with our Upstate personnel to explain how to get the matrix to work shipping from the factory. I requested that one of my model-makers bring a kid from the showroom to the meeting for them to see this doll phenomena. But the marketing personnel would not let him leave because the model-maker had put the kid in a brown bag (where the kid could have suffocated).

STORY: The Cabbage Patch Kids (called *Bok Choy Wah-Wah* in Chinese) were a huge world-wide sensation. K.W. Lee (who made the original Toy Fair Samples), was quoted *"these are the ugliest dolls I have ever seen, but I like them because they make me money, but I think the American people are crazy"*. *Kader* (Kenneth Ting) was our largest supplier at 120K/week, followed by *Perfekta* (Edmund Young) at 80K/week, then *Kam Toys* (K.W. Lee) at 30K/week. The following year, I found additional manufacturers in China, Taiwan, Japan and Spain, totaling more than 100,000 kids/day.

STORY: Kam Toys was the first manufacturer to be awarded the contract for CPK dolls. They made the (300) dolls required for the Toy Fair showroom and did an excellent job. However when they tried to mass-produce the 'one-of-a-kind' dolls, they could not do it. Finally, I met with K.W. and informed him that we were going to cancel his 400K order.

K.W. started to cry; this loss would have put him into financial ruin. I reluctantly allowed him to continue and would accept whatever he could make. Eventually, they did reach 30K kids/week.

STORY: K.W.'s son went to RPI (a year behind Eric), so I suggested that they meet in the hope that Eric would help him get adjusted to his new school. When we next had dinner together, K.W. declared that his son considered my son to be a 'playboy.' His son went on to graduate with a perfect 4.0.

The manufacture of the dolls had several difficult challenges. The rooting of hair into the vinyl heads would sometimes leave broken needles. How do we ensure that no needles were left inside the doll heads? I went to a packaging show where an equipment manufacturer was selling metal-detectors to be used in the fish industry (how about finding a fish hook in a sardine can)? So I bought some of those machines, and eventually every CPK was so tested.

Cabbage Patch Kids were a HUGE success::

(1) 800+ shoppers riot for a chance to buy CPK, four people got hurt one broken leg [Wilkes-Barre,12-83]

(2) Coleco's Cabbage Patch kids hit the top of 'The 1984 Hot Toy List' [Toy & Hobby World 2-2-84].

(3) Customers at a Toys-R-Us waited on line all night to buy one doll [Commack, NJ 11-25-83].

(4) A man paid $700 at an auction for a CPK for his daughter [Knickerbocker News 12-2-83].

(5) Cabbage Patch kid fever storm Japan at 6500 Yen [Tokyo Post 2-12-85].

(6) [8]CPK was featured on Newsweek cover [11-3-83

(7) At a burglary, a CPK was stolen and later returned to the 'mother' [Fort Meyers Press, FL 7-12-85].

(8) A 'mother' and her CPK was seen on the Great Wall of China [New York Post, NY 12-14-85].

(9) A CPK flew aboard the U.S. Space Shuttle, now resides at the Smithsonian [1985].

(10) A CPK became a mascot at the U.S. Olympic Team in Barcelona [1992].

(11) The CPK was added on a US Postage stamp [2001],

There were also many (*untrue*) stories reported:

(**1**) Coleco had a seven year supply of dolls, but are artificially creating the shortage.

(**2**) Dockside observers reported seeing freighters loaded with CPK but were not to come into port.

(**3**) Congressional sources said a bill will be introduced to create a windfall profits on CPK dolls sold.

(**4**) A 6-year old child was mugged and her CPK stolen, police artists were able to create a composite sketch of the stolen doll.

(**5**) Police in Manhattan reported that thousands of tiny runaways were jamming Port Authority terminal.

(**6**) The New England Journal of Medicine published an article stating that several Cabbage Patch Kids were unhappy with their adoptive homes and were attempting to find their natural parents.

STORY: We even had four dolls stolen out of our Wallingford home! They were sitting on top of the couch in our living room, and suddenly disappeared. One of those dolls was an Oriental doll, (one of two ever made). The thief was never found, could it have been one of our friends?

Coleco soon followed with Kids with Growing hair (made by Perfekta); Talking Kids (made by AEL and GE); and accessories like playpens, backpacks, and rockers (made at our Upstate factories).

Downhill Years 1985-88

In 1984, Coleco introduced the *ADAM Computer*. (Fortunately, I was not involved with either it's development or manufacture). It's quality was a total disaster and was one of Coleco's ultimate downfall. Eric Bromley conceived the idea of the computer as a way to use up the heavy overbought inventory of components intended for ColecoVision, (when it's sales started to decline).

In 1985, we introduced '*Sectaurs: Warriors of Simbion*'; with each hero or villain accompanied a terrifying, furry, wild-eyed insect. This was also not a great sell. Later, Coleco bought *Wrinkles* (from *Leisure Dynamics*), then *Trivial Pursuit* (from *Selchow & Righter*), then *Furskins* (from *Xavier Roberts*); but none compared with CPK success.

The next year, Coleco introduced *Alf*, and *Talking Alf*, which were manufactured by *Iljoo* in South Korea. Alf was a TV character who was a smart-mouthed creature with a bad attitude, who crash-landed in a U.S. home owner's garage. The resident family took him in. While he commented on human kind "*I'm a people alien*", he would try to catch and eat the family's cat.

124

STORY: During one of my many trips to Korea, I was given a jar of *Kim Chi* (fermented cabbage) which I loved. I decided to ship it to our CT office, together with some toy samples. When I returned, I asked my secretary where my samples were. She replied that she had thrown them away because they were covered with a 'smelly' mold.

STORY: On every business trip to Seoul, Korea, I bought a suitcase and went shopping in the *Dong Daemun* shopping center for <u>genuine</u> 'Member's Only' jackets, 'Nike' sneakers, 'Dior' handbags; all counterfeit knock-offs, of course.

STORY: On one Winter trip, I went skiing with *Erdwin Joo* and *Doug Peterson.* As Erdwin and I came skiing down the hill, Doug jokingly remarked *"Here come the two Jews"*.

In 1987, Coleco introduced *StarCom*, designed and manufactured by *Tomy*, of Tokyo, Japan. To supervise and consult with the design, I traveled frequently to Japan. While on one of those trips, Tomy was considering selling their U.S. distribution rights to either Hasbro or Coleco. I was asked by *Kantoro Tomiyama* (their CEO) which company I would recommend them to align with. Thereupon, I picked up and turned over a teacup, showing him the name imprinted on the bottom. I pointed out that if they went with Hasbro, the name TOMY would disappear off the bottom of all their toys. The next day, Tomy signed an agreement with Coleco.

STORY: Where we lived in Wallingford, I had built a Japanese garden. On one of my trips to Japan, I proudly showed a photograph of my small garden to my Japanese compatriots. They responded with an AAH, then proclaimed that it wasn't the garden that they liked, but the large lawn surrounding it!

STORY: Periodically, my vendors gave lavish dinners featuring 5-6 pound lobsters. One night, I was in my hotel room alone, and dying for some lobster. I went across the street to the *North Lake Seafood Palace* and ordered a lobster. Five pounds was the smallest they had; so that's what I ordered. Three waiters stood by my chair watching me eat that whole lobster!

STORY: When things became really bad at Coleco, we had an expat *Al Brown* who was stationed and living in Hong Kong, who got very anxious to return to the U.S. But Coleco may not pay for him, his family or for his furniture, once they filed for bankruptcy. I solved his dilemma, I sold our QA Lab equipment to *Dr. Angela Fatta* of ACTS, of Buffalo, NY, who wanted to set up a lab in Hong Kong. They made out the check to me personally, which I then passed on to Al. This transaction may not have been legal, but who cares?

126

Quality Assurance

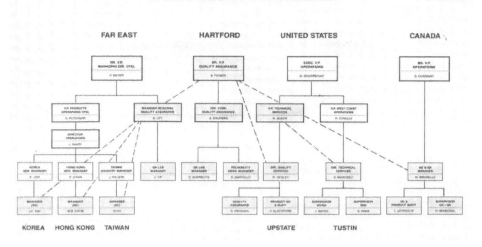

In June 1985 I was promoted to Sr. VP of Quality Assurance; and became responsible for ~200 personnel in our QC and QA organizations in Hartford, Upstate NY, Montreal, Hong Kong, China, and Korea, (see chart above).

Since I worked with both QC (Quality Control) and QA (Quality Assurance), I had often been asked what the difference was between the two? [9] Lee Iacocca (died July 3, 2019) in his book gave the best answer: "*If you bought a new car and the air conditioning did not work, that's a QC problem; if it worked but started to cool after half an hour, than that's a QA problem*".

STORY: After a QA seminar I once gave in Hong Kong, my manager *Andrew Ley* whispered to me that I had misstated something I had said. When I asked why he had not corrected me, he replied that it would have been improper for him to have corrected me in front of my staff!

127

Part 5

The Kids are Grown

◇◇◇◇◇◇◇◇◇◇◇◇◇◇◇◇◇◇

Sandy

Sandy: My charming and beautiful wife *Sandy Jay Winkler,* was born in Troy, NY, and, went to *Troy High School*: we met while I was at RPI. She later went on to *Fisher Junior College*, in Boston, MA. We got married quite early (she was 19, I was 22), so our three children followed early. It was great to be young for our eight grandchildren, which gave us a greater appreciation for them.

I traveled far away from home quite often during my working career. We made up with lots of world-wide travels together in our later years. Sandy and I have traveled extensively throughout the world (see MY VACATIONS).

Over the years, Sandy's closest friends had been *Jeri Ekholm* (née Abrams), *Sondra-Lee Nirenberg* (née Levine), *Mickey Bally* (née Jacobs), and *Louise Penta*.

For much of our early lives, Sandy had smoked daily, except during her pregnancies. I could never understand the 'urge' of smokers. Sometimes she could not get up to change the TV channels (before remotes), yet she would get up, get dressed, and drive to the grocery store, to buy a pack of cigarettes.

Sandy did not work in the early years of our marriage, as she was busy rearing our three great kids. However, as our kids got older, she worked as an employment counselor at her friend *Jeri Abrams'* at *Snelling & Snelling*. On August 4, 1985 she won the 'President's Award' for the most placements over the past several months. Later, on June 2, 1988, Sandy became a partner with *Judy Luber* to form *Jobs-R-Us,* also job recruiting.

For any of our birthday celebrations, we'd bring all the kids to the *Hu-Ke-Lau* restaurant. We often gave lavish dinner parties at home, with lots of hand-made hors d'oeuvres. We would feed the kids, then herd them upstairs 'to be seen but not heard'.

STORY: While I was overseas on business, Sandy bought a 25% share of the Jobs-R-Us building in Hamden. (She missed reading the fine print which stated that she was financially responsible for **100%** of the loan). Unfortunately, the business soured, we lost the building, which cost (our portion) $95,000, plus exorbitant legal fees.

STORY: While I was on another business trip, Sandy bought a used Mercedes convertible (required a replacement engine); and later a new Honda motorcycle. Note that this was all done while I was 9,000 miles away on business !

130

Traveling to and from China in those days was very different than when I was living there as a child. Air travel was easier too, it only took 18 hours (non-stop) from JFK to Tokyo then onto Hong Kong. Sandy and I would communicate via phone (twice/week), and via fax (daily).

Omi and Sandy often fought. While I was on one of my frequent business trips to the Far East, my mother was staying with us. Not sure whom would have been killed?

STORY: Sandy looked forward to her birthdays, often planning a 'surprise' party for herself. On one such occasion, she planned to accompany our friend *Al Winchell* on a business trip to Boston. They cancelled the trip, and instead went to the movies to see 'Goldfinger'. Several months later, she and I went to see this same movie and I was astonished when Sandy kept telling me what came next.

STORY: When our kids were grown, I decided to bring Sandy with me on a business trip, together with my mother, Caryl and Marvin. We proceeded to book our hotel and air (of course at our expense). Two weeks before our departure, my secretary had lunch with the president's secretary, when she proceeded to tell her *"what a nice thing that Bert was doing for his family"*. Then, the president *Arnold Greenberg* called me into to his office and forbad me to take my family; I went to Hong Kong, and the family went to Las Vegas!

STORY: Sandy was not fond of Arnold. During one of the annual 'bonus' parties where they passed out year-end bonuses, Sandy wanted us to sit as far away from Arnold as possible. However, just before the start of the event, Arnold moved the podium, sitting directly in front of us! Many years later, after Coleco had folded, we had dinner with *Leonard &Phyllis Greenberg*. Sandy told him some stories about Arnold, to which Leonard replied *"he is my brother"*.

In October 2016, Sandy and I were invited to *Melissa & Noah Tepperberg's* (*Susann* son's) wedding. What an affair! There were 400+ invitees at the Plaza hotel, including *Adrian Brody* (The Pianist), *Ellen Pompeo* (Grey's Anatomy), *Mario Lopez* (Extra host), *Paris Hilton* (Simple Life), and many other celebrities.

STORY: On one of our recent trips to Las Vegas, we embarked from Newark airport. As Sandy was not feeling well, I ordered her a wheelchair. As the agent came, I gave her $2.00 for delivering the chair (not knowing that she would wheel her all the way up to the gate; several miles away). Not happy with her $2.00, she gave me a *nasty* look. When we got to Security, Sandy threw up on herself; requiring the agent to bring her (while carrying one of our dogs) to the Ladies room, all for $2.00. As I had already passed through Security, TSA would not allow me to cross over to check on my wife. Finally, she and the agent came; can you imagine her look? (...I did give her another $20).

Sandy's favorite aunt and uncle were *Esther* (died December 20, 1983) and *Harvey Jacobs* (died October 3, 2003). Harvey was stationed in Germany as a dentist after the war. My favorite story that he used to tell us was about a patient he had who wore a ring prominently displaying a Swastika. He was very upset when he recognized the ring, and subsequently pulled her tooth without any Novocain. Then, as she was recovering from her excruciating pain, she exclaimed that the ring depicted a Buddhist omen.

Now that our kids have grown up, we can say that we have three **GREAT** kids, 3/3 is a big success for us... Sandy did the major part in bringing them up, but I too must have played some part in their parenting. We taught them good values and honesty, to be charitable, with good work ethics.

QUOTE: "A happy wife makes a happy life" *unknown*

Helaine, Harold and Kids

Helaine: When Helaine was in her 20s, she started what would be a very successful career working at *Multimate,* then *Ashton Tate,* then *Paperclip.* The latter was a document management company that she co-founded with two Orthodox men. Can you imagine those ultra-religious Jewish men working with a secular woman, my daughter? Helaine spent five years there, creating a profitable, public face for this company, which is still doing well today. She even appeared on the Breakfast Club, talking about Paperclip. Helaine did this while rearing her three children, and commuting to/from New Jersey. Another (but unprofitable) venture she had tried with her father, was 'Hang Ears'. Not only is she pretty, but also hard working, serious, bright, charitable, ambitious, successful, motivated and a great mother.

Then in 1996, and through the next 5 years, Helaine joined up with *Eyal Shavit* to start *AxcessNet,* a company whose mission was to identify Israeli, early-stage hi-technology companies and prepare them for merger and acquisition in the U.S. They were extremely successful.

133

Helaine then started *Women's Circle*, then *Clarity Compass*, then *Out-Of-The-Crate*. Most recently Helaine became certified as a Domestic Sexual Assault Counselor, and Internal Family Systems Therapy (IFS), for which she hopes to volunteer.

STORY: During her time at Paperclip, Helaine frequently helped me while I started Reiner Associates. In June 1989, Helaine traveled with me to the CES show in Chicago, to help me recruit some business. I was a better engineer, she was a better salesman. While on the bus on the way back to the hotel, the guy sitting next to me asked who she was, and I said "my daughter", and he, thinking she was some gal I picked up; replied *"sure she is"*.

Harold: *Harold Clifford Fischer* was born on November 1, 1962, in New Haven, CT., son of *William* (died April 10, 2014), and *Ann Fischer*. Bill had been a barber, then a realtor, and always a politician. He loved Frank Sinatra, whenever we visited Bill's home, he was always to be heard.

Harold has been my favorite son-in-law (the only one). I loved him from the first day we met, after he started dating Helaine and ate cookies out of Sandy's cookie-jar the first time he was over. Harold graduated from *UConn* and started his career in singing opera (*Amahl and the Night Visitors, Barber of Seville, Madame Butterfly*, and *Man of La Mancha*), supplemented by painting houses. That career path was cut short, when he became more successful as the Director of Sales for *PaperClip* (reporting to Helaine, VP of Sales).

STORY: As PaperClip was transitioning from DOS to Windows, Harold tried persuading me to change my computer as well. Overhearing the conversation, my mother asked: *"Why are you buying windows? Why are you spending money? What's wrong with these windows"?*

For the next 9 years Harold went on to become Account Executive of *Fujitsu Scanner Products;* then on to *Kodak.* Harold recently won a performance trip to St. Martin's. He is a great father, very charitable, good baritone and creative gardener and carpenter.

The Fischer Family

Zach: *Zachary Brian Fischer* was born on April 5, 1989, in Hamden, CT. He began his directing career the moment his younger brother could walk and talk. His best performance was as zee French Painter in the '*Beauty and the Beast*', performed to a full house. Zach went to several middle schools in Acton, MA and Hamden, CT, then graduated from Ridgefield High school. He attended the *Warner Theater Camp*, while staying with us at Lakeridge.

Zach had his Bar Mitzvah on April 20, 2003, in Acton, MA; the theme (of-course) was 'theater'. For the party, I prepared a ceramic theater-mask and playbill for each table. An Elvis impersonator performed the night before which happened to also be Helaine's 40th birthday. He can be heard on any given day practicing guitar, playing the Phantom of the Opera theme on the piano, or singing while cutting the grass at home.

Later, he won the 'Battle of the Bands' at Ridgefield High School, and taught little kids to play the guitar. Zach had also helped me assemble action-figures for REINER Associates, and had spent many weeks in New Orleans and Birmingham helping build homes for hurricane victims.

136

The following poem was written by his grandmother Nandi, on Zach's Bar Mitzvah:

To Zach, our first grandson:
You are a very special boy- You were from the start,
A sweet little toddler- With oh! So much heart.
You were ours every Friday- The weekend would start-
With Chinese food , and Little cars would be part.

It was so sad for us when Monday arrived-
To Jersey you'd go and we'd deprived.
The years flew by, your siblings arrived-
You're the best big brother they could ever derive.

The move to Acton was best for all-
Except Nandi and Pop who had to recall
The very great times when you lived so near-
Friday nights were shared, ever so dear.
Talent was there, you acted with flair-

So great to watch with pride and with care.
You've grown into manhood with honor & caring-
Pop and I will never worry how you'll be faring.
We've loved you so much, right from the start-
We will forever with all of our hearts.

Nandi and Poppy

STORY: When Zach was little, his parents lived part-time in NJ, so he spent a lot of time with us. On Fridays we would all go to the '*Hunan Restaurant*' in North Haven, a Chinese restaurant there we had a corner table reserved,

Zach was our 'first-born' grandson, and we spent a lot of time together as he was growing up. I remember him eagerly skimming through each year's Toy Fair catalogues, picking out what he wanted. Zach described his Poppi as *"quick witted, king roaster, epic needler, jolliest laugher, incredibly cultured, and eminent story teller"*.

During my many trips to China, I bought knock-off video games in the back-alley streets of Hong Kong. Zach recently stated *"..now that I am an IT professional, I find it terrifying that Poppi was buying random executable programs and tossing them into his computer; I guarantee that I had installed at least one virus on his computer, not knowing what I was doing"*.

Zach was on the Dean's list when he graduated from *UMass* in June 2011 (where his mother and uncle Dana had also graduated), with a major in Marketing and Creative Writing. While in school, he also volunteered as a tour guide for the school. Zach then went on to work at *TriTek Solutions* as a Business Analyst (only 3 days/week- that's his day job), but spends a lot of his 'free' time pursuing his musical career with his band *'Good Looking Friends'*.

138

Ari: *Ari Franklin Fischer* was born on October 5, 1993, at Yale New Haven. Ari graduated from Ridgefield, High school. He had his Bar Mitzvah on October 21, 2006 in Ridgefield; the theme was 'poker'. His parent's garage was laid out with poker tables and dealers. He graduated from UConn, where his father had also graduated. Ari studied Chemical Engineering, got his BSE, and in 2014 was a recipient (the only one in CT) of the *'Udall Scholarship'* recognizing his dedication to the Environment.

We used to call Ari 'LB' (little Bert) because we looked so much alike, and had so many similar interests. After graduation from UConn, he went on to the University of California at Berkeley to study for his PhD in Chemical Engineering, where he was granted a five year scholarship and generous stipend; he is soon to graduate in May 2020. Ari is an eminent scholar and mentor to Masters' students and underclassmen, and his research is being published.

STORY: When Ari was about three, the family was eating lobster at his home in Hamden. I took one of the live lobsters, put it on the ground, and encouraged Ari to pick it up. He was scared and replied: *"I'm only a little boy"*.

Ari loves Korea, Korean food, Korean games, Korean people, Korean culture, everything Korean; he's already been there twice.

Jordan: *Jordan Natalie Fischer* was born on December 21, 1995, in Hamden, CT. Jordan graduated from Ridgefield High School. In 2008, she had her Bat Mitzvah at *Shearith Israel Temple* in Hamden; her theme was 'Music & TV'. At each table I had prepared mini-suitcases containing cheerleaders, 'Family Guy', 'Mean Girls', 'Pirates of the Caribbean', 'The Office', 'Scrubs', 'Elmo', chocolate, shopping, and her favorite places to visit Las Vegas, Alaska, Hawaii and NYC.

In and after high school, Jordan frequently worked at *Out-Of-The-Crate* and at the *Ridgefield Animal Shelter*. Then, in college, she graduated with a BFA for animation from *Emerson College*, Boston completed in only 3 years. She became a vegetarian at age six, and is still a Vegan today. After graduation, Jordan moved to Seattle, to join *Arcadia Farms* then *EarthCorps*, made up of volunteers that develop leaders to strengthen the community and restore the health of our environment. She will soon be working teaching kids at *ALES Ecology Center* in Brooklyn.

In 2008, Sandy and I took Ari and Jordan to a trip through Alaska, via the *Alaskan Railroad*. We toured through

140

glaciers, cruised around Seward, visited an Eskimo village, and were pulled by Iditarod sled dogs. This was our best trip ever (being with our grand-children).

Jordan wrote the following letter as she was seeking a job position; this best exemplifies who Jordan is:

"When I came across this job opening, I was beyond excited. This job is an accumulation of what I care most about; nutrition, environmental education (particularly with young kids), and gardening. After graduating from college, I decided to dedicate my time to the outdoors. I volunteered with the WWOOF program where I tended to 40 animals and a large garden on the Olympic Peninsula in Washington. I spent two months there learning about composting, crop rotation, soil maintenance, and pruning, among other things. Following that, I spent a month at a perm-culture farm in Spain where I learned about pesticide-free pest control, irrigation, and water recycling. These farming experiences have greatly altered my life ever since. My passion for sustainable living and eating grew tenfold, and I knew I had to start down a career path that would let me connect to nature as much as possible.

I next began working for Earth Corps, a Seattle-based environmental restoration job sponsored by the AmeriCorps program. For 10 months, Earth Corps allowed me to spend 10 hours a day working outside in all varieties of landscapes and weather. Most days involved removing invasive species and replacing them with plants native to the Pacific Northwest. Throughout my term I also participated in a number of diverse projects, including spending a week surveying river banks for invasive plants, and another week on a boat removing poisonous debris from the ocean. Being part of protecting the earth felt amazing. A crucial part of the Earth Corps program involved a number of educational workshops and discussions on topics such as storm water infrastructure, environmental justice, gender, and land management. The third key component of the program was leading volunteer events, working side by side with students of all ages, and teaching them about the benefits of restoration. The best part was getting my hands covered in dirt.

In the past I had worked with youth and always found it so rewarding. At Out of the Crate, I was able to connect to a group of high school interns. In our group, we talked about how animals (especially dogs) can be motivators and inspiration for emotional, mental and physical well-being. I was inspired and greatly encouraged by their openness and vulnerability. I worked alongside counselors to ensure the safety of campers who required attention due to developmental disabilities.

Throughout my life I've been passionate about sustainable and healthy eating. As a child my parents raised me to be conscious of the food I eat and how it affects my body. As I grew older I became a vegan, which required me to get creative with food, which inspired my love of cooking. At the age of 15 I really learned my love of preparing healthy and delicious foods. I've worked as a chef in multiple vegan/ health conscious restaurants as well as cooked private meals for many people. I get emotional when I start thinking about how important it is for people to love the food they eat, and cooking for oneself is empowering.

This job would be an amazing way to be able to combine all the skills I've been learning over the past few years. Connecting to the earth around me is fundamental for my own mental and physical health - connecting children to gardens in their own city and learning how to utilize the gifts of the earth is so exciting to me. I can't wait to share my passion".

Eric, Gail and Kids

Eric: The commencement speaker at his graduation from the *University of New England College of Osteopathic Medicine* (as a DO doctor), was former president George H.W. Bush. Eric went on to be an intern and resident, ending up as an *Interventional Radiologist* at *Yale New Haven Hospital*; where he worked for the next 15 years. He was also Associate Professor, board certified and licensed in Connecticut, Tennessee, and Mississippi. After leaving Yale, Eric became *Director of Oncological Radiology* at West Cancer Clinic, in Memphis, TN. After a year, he left them; sold his home there, and moved back to CT. What's next in Eric's career?

Eric often helped me with REINER consulting projects, one of which was a blood-flowing device, which Eric named the *Plethysmograph* to measure the pulse for a pulse-meter, which I designed and manufactured for Precise. He also helped me with *Santa's Ski Slope*, and a toy octopus where he designed the required plumbing and piping.

143

Eric, being forever creative, proposed to Gail in a hot-air balloon. They and their kids LOVE Disney: their house is totally covered with Disney pictures, sculptures, even in their bathrooms. They travel at least twice each year (with and without their children) to visit Disneyworld, and have even been to Tokyo Disneyland (with us). Eric is bright, gentle, kind, sincere, honorable, great father and a caring doctor.

Gail: *Gail Marie Ro*che was born on May 22, 1961 in Jamaica Plains, Boston, MA. In 1985, she graduated from *Fairfield University*, then got her Master's in Social Work from *Southern Conn State University*. After college, she worked for *Connecticut Mental Health Center, Mercy Hospital, Southern Maine Medical Center, Yale University,* and *Albany Medical Center*, as a psychiatric social worker.

Gail was introduced to Eric by our good friend *Ellice Rosoff* (thanks Ellice!). As Eric was often snoring at night, Gail is forced to sleep away from him. She has been found sleeping in a bathtub, and a hotel hallway. As Gail thought that she could not have kids, Sandy and I went to China to learn how to adopt a girl; when we returned, she was pregnant

Although being Catholic, she never the less brought Aaron and Sydney up Jewish-- that's true religious tolerance! Gail is bright, hard working, sociable, and a great mother.

Gail's parents are *Timothy* (died April 26, 2017) and *Mary Roche.* Aaron and Sydney are extremely fond of their grand-parents (both sets). At one of our trips to Disney World, Sydney was seen driving Ted on his electric wheelchair, with her sitting on his lap. Mary now lives in an independent living home in Medway, MA.

QUOTE: **"If everyone is mining for gold, you will want to sell pick-axes".** *Dennis Koslowski.*

The Reiner Family

Aaron: *Aaron Jacob Reiner* was born on December 11, 1997 at Yale New Haven. He had a religious conversion at a *Mikva* because his mother remained Catholic. He went to *Ezra Academy,* and had his *Bar Mitzvah* at *Bnai Jacobs Temple*, in Woodridge, CT. In October 2013 Aaron went for a two week tour of Israel, as part of the 'Birth Right' program. He graduated from Amity High School. He loves video games, and has even taught younger students.

Aaron is now studying at the *Rochester Institute of Technology* (RIT), majoring in Video Game Technology, is due to graduate soon.

146

Sydney: *Sydney Ilana Reiner* was born on March 10, 2002, in Albany, NY. She had a religious conversion at a *Mikva* (because her mother had not converted). She went on to *Ezra Academy*, in Woodbridge; then attended *Amity High School*, where she's been busy with her Dance classes. In May 2016, Sydney too went to Israel (as part of her Ezra school program). She is due to graduate in 2020.

STORY: While I carried her when she was little, she would often play with my gold *abacus* (which I always wear around my neck). Holding it, she would give me a 'kiss' whenever I said 'aba<u>cus</u>'. We frequently visited a farm where Sydney loved petting the *Alpacas,* but was afraid to do so. (Would you believe that Alpacas are 'potty-trained'; they always do their 'job' at the same location).

147

Dana, Angela and Kids

Dana: Immediately after graduation, Dana started as Account Manager at *PaperClip* (reporting to his brother-in-law Harold), this was a great opportunity as jobs were hard to get. He did well for them, spent his next 11 years at *FileNet* (where he made a multimillion $ sale to Pepsi), then Sr. Account Executive at *IBM*, then *PegaSystems*, then *TriTek Solutions*, then *Perficient*, and presently at *RulesWare* where he was recently promoted to "Vice President of Customer Success and Strategy". For the later, he now travels extensively throughout the U.S. and Central America. Dana wrote an excellent article on *"Business Transformation"* in the prestigious *'Insights Success'* magazine (Sept 2017). Dana is very well organized (like his father), successful, fun, charming, sweet, lovable and ambitious.

STORY: On a trip the family took to Singapore, I had a voucher for 50% off on a car-rental. When Dana and I

148

proceeded to the rental agency, although the streets are very wide in Singapore, I was very nervous about driving on the 'wrong' side of the street. When I got to Avis, I was informed that they would not accept my voucher. I said OK, and Dana and I left, thankful for an excuse not to drive there.

STORY: As a college graduation present, we took Dana with us to Israel and Rome. While in Jerusalem, Dana and his cousin *Liat Cohen* had tickets to see *Elton John* at a venue in Tel Aviv. It turned out that the concert was canceled, so I awoke Dana to show him the newspaper headlines, but of course, he thought I was joking!

STORY: On a later trip, the whole family traveled to Disney World. Dana had had a strained ankle playing basketball (I didn't think he was tall enough to play), so we rented a wheel-chair. One night we had dinner at the Japanese Pavilion, when we got out, someone had stolen it.

Dana proposed to Angela at the neighborhood *Stop'n Shop*. He had them announce over the speaker for her to meet him at aisle 5 (the candy aisle, as she loves candy!). When she arrived, squeezing past the throngs of onlookers, Dana was on his knee with her ring in his hand.

Angela: *Angela Ann Teresa Vigilotti* was born on November 1, 1971 in Staten Island, NY. In 1989, she got her Bachelor's Degrees in English and French from *Drew University*, in Madison, NJ. After graduation she worked at *PaperClip*, where she and Dana met. She then went on to work at *Synapse*, then *Cushman & Wakefield*, then *Mercer* Inc. She is an accomplished writer, having authored '*You Can't Dance in Those Pants*' and '*Skin Deep Series*'. Angela is pretty, creative, PC knowledgeable (always ready to help me... not always), great cook, and a loving mother.

STORY: During Dana and Angela's wedding reception, her grand-mother *Concetta Fasano* (died March 30, 2003) was approached by the DJ for her to speak into the microphone to express good wishes to the newly married couple. She grabbed the mic holding it to her ear, thinking it was a telephone.

Angela's parents are *Phyllis* (died January 4, 2000) and *Ralph Vigilotti*. Angela and Dana were married on June 13, 1998 at the *Glen Island Club*, New Rochelle, NY (formerly the Glen Miller Casino). Tragically, her mother Phyllis passed away shortly thereafter, at an early age of only 57.

She is widely known as the 'family IT Person', she helps me, Helaine, and even Dana with all our computer problems. Angela, being a devout Catholic, made Sandy and I understand that she would not give up her religion after they got married. Angela and Dana agreed that they would bring up their children accordingly. We acknowledged, so, we now have three wonderful Catholic grandkids who follow their mother's beliefs; we are very OK with that.

The Reiner Family

150

Philip: *Philip Jackson Reiner* (affectionately known as PJ) was born on June 13, 2004, in Sleepy Hollow, NY. PJ is a most generous child: he had emptied and sent his whole piggy-bank to help Haiti Relief efforts. When he was little, with his mischievous grin, he overheard Harold calling Helaine *'Honey'*, thinking that was her name, he and his siblings still call her Honey to date. He had his Confirmation on May 25, 2019. Always eager to help, he will be joining the *Appalachia Service Project* this summer. PJ loves playing baseball (he's mighty good at it), also skiing and bowling. PJ wants to become a therapist when he grows up.

Lucas: *Lucas Oliver Reiner* was born on December 28, 2006, in Sleepy Hollow, NY. Lucas is now collecting coins. I hope he will take over my collections some day. He loves skiing taking after his father, and travels to VT whenever they can. At age 9, as part of a school project, Lucas wrote a book entitled "The Underground Shark". I think he's going to be an engineer, like his grandfather.

Ava: *Ava Marlowe Reiner* was born on May 20, 2011, in Sleepy Hollow, NY. (the same date as Sandy's mother).

For her 5th birthday, I built her a doll house, which I made from a kit. It's a two bedroom villa, complete with furniture, kitchen and bathroom. I loved building it. The toughest part was the roof with 512 individually colored tiles.

Ava loves animals (all kinds). Unfortunately both of her brothers are allergic, so she can't have any, except for '*Mr. Blubberton*', her Siamese Fighting fish. (Hopefully another child doesn't poison it like I did when I was a kid!).

She loves gymnastics, skiing and to play arcade driving games; not surprisingly, she wants to become a vet when she grows up.

QUOTE: "There are two things that are infinite, the universe and man's stupidity...I am not sure about the universe". *Albert Einstein*

153

Our 35th

In June 1995, for our 35th anniversary, our kids planned a trip to Hawaii. We stayed at the *Royal Hawaiian*, in Honolulu, affectionately known as the *'Pink Palace'*. Sandy and I had a great time traveling throughout the island.

We were fairly fit in those days, so we ventured to climb *Diamond Head* volcano. We drove to the caldera (the flat inside of the volcano), then climbed to the top of the mountain, which was extremely steep and difficult to climb. At the bottom we saw vendors selling water at $9.00 per bottle, which we thought was ridiculous, why would anyone pay that? Coming down the exhaustive climb, we bought water at $9.00.

QUOTE: "Out of clutter find simplicity, out of discord find harmony, out of difficulty lies opportunity" *Albert. Einstein*

Our 40th

In June 2000, for our 40th anniversary, our kids treated us to a weekend at *Top Notch Spa*, in Stowe, VT. Our three children and all our grand-kids were there. Helaine wrote and read the following beautiful poem, Sandy and I cried:

> "All three of your children and their spouses decided,
> To do something special for you that coincided,
>
> With a special date we won't soon forget,
> It happened 40 years ago, 4 years after you first met.
>
> Maybe a big bash with your new Torrington friends,
> On second thought that's not an appealing new trend.
>
> So what could we do that would really shine...
> Maybe a little quality time together would be fine.
>
> All 6 kids & 4 grandchildren planned a weekend together,
> For two days of love and laughter no matter the weather.
>
> We're all here at the beautiful Spa at Top Notch
> Getting facials or pedicures... oh how posh.

Yet now that we're here it seems crystal clear,
Something is definitely missing I fear...

I believe it's a poem written for our special events,
But that's usually Mom's creativity spent.

So here goes...we give you this gift with great affection,
To be read aloud by someone with projection.

Let's start at the end and work our way back...
You've created a loving and successful family...on track.

Mom was a housewife and spent much time in her room,
Waiting for Dad to come home hopefully soon.

All three kids felt secure knowing mom was home in bed,
We'd join her after school, watching TV for hours on end.

And when Mom decided to make dough going to work,
She became top of her game in the recruiter's network.

She won an award and rose to the top,
Then went into business with Judy and opened shop.

Dad was famous in our neighborhood, and cousins too,
Making toys year after year we never had too few.

We can remember Dad especially on long car rides,
Telling us elaborate stories of the bible or his family tribe.

Some weekends we'd join Dad at COLECO till three,
We'd eat junk food, Mom would call aunt Caryl for free.

Mom & Dad you taught us right from wrong, to be kind,
You've also showed us by doing how we certainly find,

That we're all successful with all that we've done,
Because you showed us the way through tough and fun.

156

You reinforced in each of us your hopes and desires,
Then inspired and encouraged us without tire.

Through your kind and strong words and actions,
We blossomed and sought out our very different passions.

You also taught us that life is not always fair,
But that we could excel no matter what our unique flare.

And that we should be responsible and generous people,
To our family and friends that make up our steeple.

As you can see your 40 years of highs and lows,
Is now being recited in some amateur prose....

We're so delighted you met and married 40 year ago,
And we're here to tell you we love you both so.

Thanks Mom and Dad for giving us all that you did,
You can see the real benefits through our family shindig.

Eric the cook will prepare a nice dinner,
Gail will share in the clean up, for that she's the winner.

Dana and Angela will entertain us for sure,
A little joke and an accent make them the evening cure.

As usual we expect your grandkids will steal your heart,
And we all know those little munchkins are the best part"

QUOTE: "If there are discussions you have been avoiding, that's the one you should be having". *Lee Iacocca*

QUOTE: "Be ever ready to learn, be tolerant, be broad minded". *Horace Reiner.*

Our 50th

In June 2010, for our 50th anniversary, our kids treated us to a weekend at *Mohonk Mountain Spa*, in New Paltz, NY; all our kids and grandkids were there. Helaine wrote and read to the group the following:

"How do you know if your 50 year union was successful?

When you enter into a marriage, you dream of having a family and hope that generations later your values, beliefs and traditions are reflected and respected. In my opinion, this might be the best indicator of success, so on this momentous occasion, your 50th wedding anniversary, let's evaluate how you did. Let's start by reviewing what you both valued most, which probably is the reason you chose each other in the first place:

1. Family and dear friends
2. Respect
3. Kindness/compassion/generosity
4. Education, working hard
5. Pride and being proud of those you love

6.   Tradition-celebration with food as an integral component
7.   Love of animals
8.   Open and accepting of others
9.   Being honorable
10.   Laughter and enjoying life especially with those you love

If these are some of the values you deem as most important, in order to successfully transfer them to your 3 children, you would have had to show us not just tell us. (Walk the walk, not just talk the talk). And you did.

You taught us respect. To respect ourselves, our parents, our teachers, our siblings. You respected your parents, and even though at times it was challenging, out of respect you did the right thing-like the time Dad had to apologize to Papa for insulting Nana's lamp. Or the number of times Nandi schlepped to see Omi when she really didn't want to.

You also took such pride in your children and still do. You may show us how proud you are by announcing an accomplishment in the Reiner newsletter, or we may see it your eyes when a grandchild does something kind.

Family and dear friends were always a priority-whether we'd travel hours to spend Passover in Buffalo with Aunt Caryl and Uncle Marve or drop everything when a friend or family member was in need. We saw this over and over again, from Susan's Benji's unexpected death at 3; and also to supporting Nate and Iris through their most difficult illnesses.

We learned compassion through you opening your home to those who might be lonely during a holiday or witnessing you invite Louise, Jeri, Vicki, Iris, Joan to join you somewhere. They never felt like 3rd wheels in your company. All Jewish holiday celebrations at your house became standing room only events, primarily because you wouldn't leave anyone out.

159

If you weren't inviting people in need to your home, then you might be catching a stray cat or dog and providing shelter. Or did you intentionally steal the Hood's cat? We always knew that kindness to animals was important. You love animals as much as your kids, and probably some days a little more. Being loving to animals was natural for both of you.

But what happened when one of your children wanted you to be loving and accepting...and it wasn't so natural? When it counted the most, you rose to the occasion. First with Harold then Gail and then Ang. What seems like a distant memory, because your in-law kids mean as much to you as your own kids, was really a true test of you being accepting and open. What a wonderful lesson, because in each case, even though not one of them was born Jewish, they all manifest the values and virtues you admire most. Your 3 children all chose mates that share the values I mentioned earlier.

Now the true test is, were we able to instill these values in our kids? Let's take it grandchild by grandchild:

Zach –Your first grandchild, who always had so much talent and charisma as a youngster (making friends wherever he went) we weren't quite sure if he would turn out to be one of those egotistical, superficial musician types. We quickly saw the depths of his charitable nature and kind, sincere heart when he went to New Orleans. He was saddened by what he saw, and the following year he managed to scrape together the funds and become group leader so he could help out again. We see it every day when he won't miss a family function, or the way he'll drop everything when someone he loves needs him.

Ari-we used to call him LB because he and Poppy looked so much alike. Ari loves kids as much as poppy does, and as we all know, he has always been kind and gentle to his younger cousins and little sister-they love him and he genuinely adores them. Ari has made so many good choices throughout high school-based on many of the values you instilled in us, such as doing well in school as evidenced

160

in his tremendous grades. More importantly, he's managed to keep the moral high ground during high school, which is not easy these days. He aspires to have a solid career so he can have as many TV's as you do!

Jordan-loves animals as much as you both do. She is a girl of action-not just words, we are very well aware of her vegetarian diet. She's also compassionate toward people in need as well-as evidenced by the work she's done for the well project. Jordan is also kind, for example when Ari didn't want to go to Europe for vacation with us because he knew he wouldn't enjoy it (he didn't want us to waste the money) Jordan immediately said they should both stay home-even though she really wanted to go, but didn't want to leave Ari behind.

Aaron- is a very hard worker. Sometimes it takes him a little longer to get his work done, but he will work until it's done right. That's the education/hard working value on steroids. And Aaron is considerate and respectful as well. In second grade, when the class was doing a project, they had to wait until everyone was done before going out to recess. Aaron approached his teacher and said that it wasn't fair that all of the other kids had to wait for him because he took longer than others and offered to stay in for recess to finish up while all the others went outside. The teacher let everyone including Aaron go then. If you ask my kids, they will tell you this is typical of Aaron, he always wants to make sure everyone is included...and will give up doing what he wants to so everyone can be happy.

Sydney- family comes first. She cried for several nights before Aaron left for camp because she was going to miss him and being the awesome brother he is, he kept hugging her to reassure her. The Monday before he left for camp he had his tooth pulled and Sydney cried because she didn't like to see her brother hurt, and she slept next to him in his room on the floor in her sleeping bag "in case he needed anything in the night". Sydney's not just fond of her big brother, she loves her whole family. As Ari had witnessed, Sydney will play what Lucas wants to play, even if she prefers something else.

161

PJ-When his Kindergarten class learned about the hurricane in Haiti, it also coincided with a lesson about making wishes. He came home from school with a colored-in picture of a rainbow and a wish to be able to send money to the people in Haiti. As Ang opened his book bag she asked him to explain his picture and wish. As he was describing it, she could see the thought light up his mind and then he shouted out, "I know, I can send my piggy bank to Haiti." So they emptied his whole bank (which he was saving for a trip to Atlantis) and headed over to the bank to convert his change into dollars which he donated to Haitian Relief efforts. Since then, he has been avidly working to refill his piggy bank and was asking his mom and dad when he would be going to Atlantis again. Ang explained that we would have to wait until the rainy season ended because it is very wet and rainy there this time of year and there can also be hurricanes and he said, "Mom, we should help them." Confused, she said, "Help them with what?" and he replied, "They need our help because of the rain." He had misunderstood a seasonal rainy season for a natural disaster and was willing to empty his vacation fund again to help people who he thought were in need.

Lucas-Before Zach's welcome home dinner, Ang told Lucas and PJ everyone would be at my house. Both kids were excited. "Will Jordan be there?" they asked. "Will Ari be there?" "What about Aaron and Sydney?" "And Zach?" Lucas said, "I can't wait to go to Honey's. Can we go right now?" to which they responded, "We know you can't wait to go to Honey's to see your cousins. We'll be going in a little while." Lucas smiled that little mischievous grin and said, "I love my cousins but I love to go to Honey's because she has junk food!" We better look up the definition of junk food. He's quite a character that one. He makes us all laugh just the same way Dana did when he was that age, and Angela does now!

To conclude the evaluation of whether or not your 50 year union will result in successfully transferring your values, beliefs and traditions, I think the answer is an overwhelming YES.

If it weren't for your uniting, we would not be here today."

162

Israel

Israel is regarded by Jews, Christians and Muslims as their biblical Holy Land. Within Jerusalem's Temple Mount resides the *Wailing Wall* (Jew's holiest site, the remains of the 2nd Herod's Temple), the *Church of the Holy Sepulchre* (where Christ was buried), the *Dome of the Rock* (where Isaac was to be sacrificed, and Mohamed ascended to heaven), and the *Al-Aqsa Mosque* (Islam's 3rd holiest site).

My aunt, *Ilse Esther Cohen* (died May 17, 2008), was my mother's younger sister. She immigrated to Israel as part of a youth Zionist group from Germany, in about 1938. My uncle *Yitzhak Cohen* (died May 18, 2015) was a 5th generation *Sabra*. They met at the *Maaoz-Haim Kibbutz* where Yitzhak was the mayor. He and Ilse got legally married on February 7, 1939 when they both were 22 years old, but had said their vows (secretly) several years earlier.

Sandy and I have made several trips to Israel (in '80, '93, '98, '08, '14), as did Helaine, Harold, Zach, Ari, Jordan, Dana, Aaron and Sydney. We have been to most ancient and modern sites in Jerusalem, Tel Aviv and Haifa. We have visited *Yad Vashem* (Holocaust museum), climbed *Masada* (the fortress where 967 Jews committed suicide in 73 AD), toured the *Baha'i* temple (World Center of Baha'i faith), walked the *Stations of the Cross* (the path where Jesus walked on the way to his crucifixion), and rode camels; we did it all.

On October 2, 1980 we took our first trip to Israel, together with *Caryl* and *Marve, Phyl* and *Bill*. The following are some excerpts of my notes I had taken during that trip:

Day 1: We have arrived in *Eretz Israel*. After all the years that I had said *"Next year in Jerusalem"*, we are finally here.

Day 2: We travel to the cultural center of Tel Aviv. On our left is the *Helena Rubenstein Pavilion*, and behind it is the beautifully landscaped *Gan Yaacov* (Jacob's Garden). On the right is the *Habimah National Theater*, home of the Israeli Philharmonic Orchestra. Further down the beach you can view the panorama of the Tel Aviv shore and beach.

Day 3: Old Jaffa, where we are now, is a city that's 6,000 years old, one of the oldest in the world. Here took place the fight of the Crusaders against Jerusalem. Napoleon also tried to capture it. Towards the end of the Ottoman Empire, Jews fled the pogroms from Eastern Europe and Russia coming here, this was known as the first *'Alija'*.

Day 4: We are on a mini-bus traveling south to *Yammit* in the Negev (a city which will be turned over to Egypt in '82, a condition signed between *Begin* and *Sadat* during the *Camp David Accord*. Next we visit the kibbutz *Yad Mordechai*, located on the border of the Gaza Strip, in which the *War of Independence* of '48, the *Six Day War* of '67, and again during the *Yom Kippur War* of '73, was the scene of intense battles and also the victories.

164

Day 5: First we come to *Megiddo*. Archeologists have unearthed the remains of about 20 cities, one built on top of the other. They include temples from King David and King Solomon. Also found were tunnels to feed them water, this ingenious engineering feat enabled those inside to withstand long sieges. The next stop is *Kibbutz Deganya*, this was Israel's first kibbutz, today they happen to be celebrating their 70th anniversary. As we leave, we notice a Syrian tank that was demolished in 1948. We see young soldiers hitch-hiking, and everywhere remnants of abandoned tanks.

Day 6: We have now traveled north along the *Sea of Galilee*, to Tiberius. We stay at a beautiful hotel located at the fresh-water lake. It is fed by the Jordan River, and is Israel's main source of water. We went swimming, what a feeling that Abraham bathed here 4,000 years ago, and as where St. Peter was baptized.

Day 7: Today we come to Zefat, one of Israel's four holy cities. The tempo of life is decidedly religious. The *Shulkhan Aruch* (Book of Jewish Law) was written here. We visited several beautifully adorned synagogues; finely carved around the *bimah* (pulpit) and beautifully painted dome ceilings. Today we celebrated *Marve* and *Caryl's* 25th wedding anniversary.

Day 8: We cross the Jordan River into the *Golan Heights,* (now too dangerous to visit). This area, bordering Syria, was captured in 1967. We see its strategic importance to Israel. (One of the pictures I took was of a defense bunker, which I later posted on my office wall. When people would ask me what its significance was, I replied that in the U.S. no one had ever built, nor have seen any). We see the T.A.P. oil pipeline, which crosses Saudi Arabia, Jordan, Syria and Israel before reaching Lebanon. We are guarding this pipeline for the Arabs?

165

Day 9: Next we pass *Tel Hai*, this was the hill where in 1920 only eight defenders including the one-armed *Joseph Trumpeldor*, died defending this hill against the Arabs. This had a special meaning to me, because as a boy in China, I had belonged to *Betar*, the Zionist organization named after him, '*Brit Trumpeldor*'.

Day 10: Next we arrive at Haifa, this lush city and sea-coast, is located on a hill overlooking the Mediterranean. We first visit the *Baha'i Shrine*; it's golden dome is the landmark of Haifa. Founded in Persia, it's prophets include Abraham, Moses, Christ, Buddha, Mohammed and Bahaullah; embracing the unity of all religions. The gardens surrounding the temple are beautifully and geometrically landscaped, creating a world, serenely remote, encouraging meditation. This port was widely used by illegal escapees after Europe's holocaust, when Britain turned these immigrants to Cyprus & Mauritius.

Day 11: We then toured a Carmel Winery. Then on to *Caesarea*, built by King Herod in 22 BCE. We see the ruins of a Roman amphitheater and aqueduct which traveled water for 20 miles. These are ruins from 2,000 years ago, and in its midst a kiosk selling 'Coca-Cola'.
All around we see even rows of trees, planted by JNF

Day 12: At last we reach *Yerushalayim* (Jerusalem). From the occupation in 1948, through to the six day war, Jews were excluded to enter. We rush to the *Ha-Kotel Ha-Ma'aravi* (Wailing Wall). This is the only remains of the Second Temple destroyed in 70 BCE. The entrance is heavily guarded, all packages and pocketbooks are thoroughly searched before entry. Standing here, I felt a mixture of awe and strangeness. Every synagogue in the world faces Jerusalem, and here I stand. People are praying, standing facing this wall; but should Jews be actually praying to a wall?

166

Day 13: Holy to Jews, Christians and Muslims (Jerusalem is mentioned in the Bible 700 times, but not once in the Koran). We are trying to check into the Hilton hotel, but, no rooms! We're in luck, Caryl and Marve and we get checked into the 'King Saul' suite. It's fantastic with five balconies, dining room, kitchen and sauna, on the 19th floor overlooking the old city. We then toured the *Dome of the Rock* (where Abraham was about to sacrifice Isaac), the *Al Aqsa Mosque* (Islam's 3rd holiest shrine), the Church of the *Holy Sepulcher*, (where Christ was buried). We walked the *Via Dolorosa* (where Christ walked on his way to his crucifixion). We then went onto the Hadassah Hospital to view the Chagall Windows. **What a great trip we all had!**

STORY: The U.S. Embassy was located in Tel Aviv. Finally in 2018, president Trump moved the U.S. Embassy to Jerusalem, the Israeli capital (the only good thing that Trump ever did). On one of our trips, we needed a large box to ship one of our souvenirs. Sandy went to the Tel Aviv embassy, next door to the Sheraton, to ask for a box; she's got guts!

Rotem (Amit's) is now in the IDF (*Israeli Defense Forces*); hope she does well in defending her country. My cousins now living in Israel (except *Liat* & her family) are:

Eytan & Marcella Cohen---Amit & Tovah--- Lahav+Rotem+Eden

Liat & Eretz Gold--- Shira+Assaf+Yotam

Ohad & Ruth Cohen---Ma'ayan+Shahar

Uri & Revital Cohen----   Gilad & Ester Cohen---Ye'ela+Itamar

Ayelet & Itay Levi--- Gal+Shay+ Ron

Udi Cohen

167

Our Pets

Growing up in China, my pets were crickets (taught to box), Japanese beetles (string-tied to watermelon rind), snakes (red-ring-necked racer), baby alligator (had to wear gloves to handle), lizards (chameleon), frogs, salamanders, turtles, and fresh-water fish; but no dogs. Later, after we married, we had a rabbit (*Hopper*), a guinea pig (was put down for fear that she had contaminated Helaine with Typhoid fever), a cat (*Tiger*), and lots of salt-water fish.

Betta: We even bred a *Siamese fighting fish*. It was amazing to watch: After a male completed building a nest of bubbles, and the female was fat laden with eggs, they were ready to breed. The male wraps his body around hers, squeezes a few eggs out of her, picks them up the eggs in his mouth (to fertilize), and deposits them into the nest. This is repeated dozens of times until the female has released all her eggs, almost dead from exhaustion. I would then separate the two. From then on, the male would guard the nest; each time a few eggs dropped out, he would pick them up in his mouth and redeposit them into the nest. After a few months, we had to put each infant fish into separate baby-food jars.

Our first dog (don't remember his name?), was a German Shepherd puppy whom we bought in a pet store in Manhattan. NEVER buy a dog from a pet store. This dog was seriously ill and survived only a few weeks.

Spooky: He came next, a rescued *Weimaraner* who was about one year old. He was very sweet, but looked spooky- with yellow eyes. Spooky refused to be alone, he jumped out of our 2nd floor window; out the window of our moving car on Boston avenue; and crashed through several screen doors. We finally gave Spooky away to a girl who lived on a farm in Canada. He loved her and the freedom of that ranch; they both ended happy.

STORY: Although he was very peaceful, he did bite me once. A stray dog came into the yard and attacked Spooky. As I was afraid of him getting hurt, I reached over to grab his collar, and he (mistakenly) bit my hand.

Leibschen: (means 'lover' in German) came soon thereafter; an AKC pedigreed *German Shepherd*, whom we had gotten directly from the breeder. She was our greatest and most beloved dog. However, she was afraid of little children, having bitten (fear-biter) half a dozen of Helaine's child-hood friends. When we first got her as a puppy, she was afraid to stay alone in the same room with Helaine (who was at age one when we got Leibschen). As was recommended by our Vet *Dr. Nezvesky*, we left her alone with Helaine out on the front lawn; Leibschen started to run away, but turned around and went back to sit next to her. They then became very protective of her. She did bite several kids, including *Amy Herzlich,* whose parents became our best friends. Leibschen passed her Obedience Training, and was entered in several dog shows (but never won). She was with us till she reached the age of 13.

While we had Leibschen, we also had a rabbit named *Hopper.* She escaped after she ate through her cage/carpet.

Mac & Schnitzel: *Mac* was a huge *Scottish Deerhound*, and *Schnitzel* was a *Miniature Schnauzer*. What a contrast in size. Schnitzel generally stood between Mac's legs. It was a sight to see!

STORY: During one of my mother's visits, she was baby-sitting and Schnitzel escaped. Omi ran over to Carol's for help, they both ran through the rain trying to catch her.

171

Alex: Next came Alex a *Doberman Pincher*; the friendliest, most loving (but scariest looking) dog we ever had. She lived with Schnitzel looking after her like a mother. The breeder we got her from, was the Connecticut State Medical Examiner. We later found out that she got fired because she would do her autopsies with her Dobermans (including Alex's mother) running around the floors, liking up the cadaver's blood.

Tiger: The *Hood's* were our neighbor, they had a cat called *Tiger*, who would frequently sachet in front of our fence and antagonize our dogs. When the Hood's moved to Florida, they abandoned Tiger and left her to wander in the neighborhood. Later, in the middle of winter, we heard her pitiful cry, and found her loaded with ice and snow. We took her in. I took the dog's crate loaded with foam insulation, added a heat-lamp, and made that her home. But, when it got even colder, we brought her into our house, and surprisingly Alex and Schnitzel both loved her. Tiger was an outdoors cat, Alex would not go to sleep till Tiger was safely at home.

Gizmo: Next was *Gizmo* (our first *Norfolk Terrier*), who loved to watch TV (see above as she's watching a Cooking show). She was a great breed, was extremely friendly who, loved all our kids.

George & Gracie: Then came *Gracie* another *Norfolk Terrier*; followed by *Georgie* an *Affenpincher*, which in German means 'monkey dog'. Not sure if they are named after his face or his antics. [Does anyone remember 'George Burns and Gracie Allen']? Gracie loved everyone, but Georgie was definitely Sandy's. He was extremely loyal to her, biting anyone who came near her. Both dogs were greatly loved by us. Gracie died at home at age 13, and Georgie at the vet's at age 14.

STORY: Gracie loved to run around the *Lakeridge* neighborhood trying to catch chipmunks and rabbits, never catching any, while Georgie stayed and protected our home. We often could not find her. She would be sleeping behind the TV or hiding in a closet.

George & Gracie II: Although we vowed not to get any other dogs, it wasn't long before we got another *Gracie* (same names would make it easier to remember), born December 14, 2014 at a Las Vegas breeder, a *Maltipoo* (Maltese and Poodle mix). Then followed with *George* (a *Yorkshire Terrier*) born

June 7, 2016. Gracie does not love all (but LOVES Helaine and Kim); whereas George loves everyone.

STORY: Sandy was set on getting a '*Yorkie*', so she found a breeder on the internet. Their credentials and breeding sounded excellent. So we took Gracie along and drove down to Brooklyn. To our shock, it was a 'puppy mill', not a breeder. We wanted to turn back home, but he was so CUTE...

When we're in CT, *Kim Foster Isberg* is our dog sitter. When we're in Las Vegas, it's *Elaine Robillard*. Both dogs LOVE both sitters. When I pet George, Gracie will cry for me; when I pet Gracie, George will nestle in between us.

I've always wanted to get a parrot. Before we bought Gracie, I almost bought a 4 month old *African Grey* parrot (they have the largest vocabulary); but I decided against it because (1) they are very possessive; if Sandy would come over to kiss me, he might attack her, (2) they live 40-60 years, we would have to designate who would get him long after we're gone, (3) very noisy, (4) very destructive. My solution? I frequently go to a nursery to visit *Delilah* (a yellow-crested Cockatoo), with whom we talk.

STORY: A man wanted an exotic pet, so he went to the pet-shop and bought a Talking Centipede. He was very excited and could hardly wait to show his friends. He got dressed and urged his pet to hurry.. But no response... He asked *"what's taking you so long?"* Finally the centipede replied..."*I'm putting on my shoes*"...

QUOTE: "Today is the tomorrow you worried about yesterday". *Unknown*

Our Homes

Bridgeport: In 1960, after we married, Sandy and I moved into our first home which was an apartment at *203 Pennsylvania Ave,* in Bridgeport, CT. We lived here while I worked at *Sikorsky Aircraft,* in Stratford. On the floor below us, lived *Phil* and *Marie Abrams,* whose daughter *Jeri* remained good friends of ours; and later partnered with Sandy. I drove a '51 Chevy which I inherited from my father, then upgraded to a '61 Plymouth station-wagon. We now drove in luxury!

STORY: Phil was a salesman selling Wear-Ever cookware, Austrian crystal, and International silverware. So, I decided to try to make some extra bucks. At night I would visit homes (leads given to me by Phil) selected where there was a daughter about to be married. I did not do well selling, but I did make one sale. But, later they changed their minds and demanded their money back, which I refused to do. They took me to Small-claims court. I lost, and had to give them their back the money, and was told that *"I used high pressure sales on them"*, **Me, high pressure??**

STORY: A year after we were married, Sandy and I spent a week at Phil's cabin in Peterborough, Canada. One night, I took their rowboat and my dog Spooky, on a ride around the lake. Shortly after we embarked, a storm arose, with buckets of rain, thunder and lightning coming down on us. It was extremely scary, even Spooky was shivering. Trying to return to shore, I could not get the outboard to start, and on board was only one oar, I wasn't going anywhere. Finally, we heard another boat, I yelled for HELP, and we were safely towed ashore; was a scary experience!

Sometime a year later, Sikorsky workers went on strike for eleven weeks. Sandy was nervous driving me to work as picketers yelled and called us 'Scabs' thru the picket line.

STORY: One New Year's eve we celebrated with our neighbor's in their apartment. After several drinks, I fell asleep and dropped a bag of potato chips onto their floor. They were so pissed, they would not talk to us for several months thereafter.

STORY: Each Passover we would drive to Buffalo to celebrate with *Caryl* and *Marve*, their parents, and our children. On one such occasion, I tried to be of help by defrosted their refrigerator (with a knife). I ruptured the freezer coils and had to buy them a new one!

Hamden: After I changed jobs, we moved to *42 Ridge Road,* Hamden, CT, next to the beautiful, well-manicured, *Pardee Rose Gardens*. We lived there for two years until we got 'kicked' out. We were told by the landlord to either get rid of our dog Leibschen, or move out. Not willing to part with our dog, we obviously moved!

STORY: We did not have a basement, but a small storage space, just big enough to lay out an HO train set. I built the terrain, track, bridges, houses with lights and even a lake. One day, the son of our neighbor *Marty Breecher* was so enthralled watching the trains, he peed on the floor while watching the trains go around.

My father's closest friend (whom he had met onboard ship going to Shanghai) was *Irwin DeJong*. He was an extremely talented artist whose profession was to repair and restore valuable stamps. He was responsible for my father and me getting interested in stamp-collecting. He also had painted a copy of a Van Gogh's 'Sunflowers'. When Irwin died (October 12, 1993), I inherited that painting.

Pond Hill: In October 1964, we bought our first home, at *21 Blakeslee Road,* in Wallingford. It was a beautiful home, but our realtor (Gordon's father-in-law) neglected to tell us that we had a serious water problem! Although we had two sump-pumps our (finished) basement often covered with 10" of water covering our carpeted floor.

Our house grew as our family grew. We had built expansions to our house three separate times. Our three kids were born and raised here, where we lived happily for 37 years. We kept our kitchen 'Kosher', although we did eat

'*Treff*' in the basement and patio. In our basement, I had built a waterfall, which was so huge it could not be taken out when we moved. During the years we lived here, some of our best friends were: *Nate* (died August 4, 1995) & *Iris Goldstein* (died September 22, 1998), *Bobby* (died September 7, 2018) and *Ellice Rosoff*, and *Harold & Carol Herzlich* (who became our best friends when they too moved only 15 minutes from us in Las Vegas).

STORY: During one Thanksgiving dinner-party given by the *Herzlich's*, my mother and I mistakenly went into their next door neighbor *Ted Weiner's* house. Standing around their living room, I could not understand why Carol and Harold were not there?

STORY: Driving home, passing Bridgeport, I would buy our meat from *Bennie Levine's Butcher*; who was both Kosher and also cheaper. I would bring meat for the *Herzlichs* as well. Bennie would always have a hot corned-beef sandwich prepared for me. His assistant, who was twice my age, would load up my trunk.

STORY: We were very close to our neighbors *Camille* (died May 9, 2018) and *Dick Canny*. There was an incident when Dick was driving in New Jersey, where a paneled truck advertising a Jewish deli, cut him off. Dick yelled to him "*... you should have been killed in the camps*". I refused to talk with Dick for several months, until he finally wrote me an apology. Another incident was when we went to the Empire State Building with our boys. I had paid full fare for Eric, but Dick lied and paid children's prices (even though *Robert* and *Ricky* were well over 12); again we didn't talk.

STORY: While skiing at *Mount Southington*, I followed *Justin Barle* (son of dear friends *Lou* (died August 18, 2013) and *Joan Barle*, down an icy, treacherous '**CLOSED**' trail, slipped on the ice, and dislocated my shoulder. While in

179

severe pain and completely alone, I was able to pull myself up from a tree branch, then crawled down to meet the main trail, was then carried down by the Ski-patrol via stretcher into the hospital. The following Monday I went to work wearing a sling; my CEO Leonard Greenberg reprimanded me for skiing, saying that *"an executive of his company should not engage in such dangerous activities"*.

In 1965, Sandy's cousin *Eve Jacobs*, had had a severe car accident, when she bent down to pick up her dog who had fallen off the seat. When we went to visit her in the hospital, she was so completely bandaged, we could not recognize her.

STORY: Our next door neighbor *Helen Meckley* (died April 21, 2003) was a bitch. She wouldn't speak to either of us, or even acknowledge our kids. We came home one night in the Winter, to find the police in our driveway, answering a call from Mrs. Meckley that some snow had been willfully shoveled onto her side of the driveway.

STORY: At a neighborhood party given at *Jack Doyle's* (died October 23, 2015) house, *Al Meckley* (always friendly to us) asked Sandy to dance. When his wife Helen saw them dancing, she screamed and stormed out of the house. I wonder what happened at their home later that night?

STORY: When I started my business *REINER Associates* in our garage, Mrs Meckley complained to the Wallingford Zoning Board of impending noise (by my computers).With the help of Harold's father *Bill Fischer*, I won.

STORY: Coming back a day early from our trip from Las Vegas; our dog was still at the kennel. We had left the front door unlocked (it was a safe neighborhood), and the car was parked in the driveway. That night, a policeman (*Ed Gerosa*) came to inspect the house, walked up the stairs and

180

scared us to hell when we were confronted. He shined his flashlight on himself, so that I might not shoot him in error. (Ed later married our friend Camille).

STORY: Together with our neighbor *Ky Nastri* (died May 29, 2017), and all of our kids, we drove to *Jungle Habitat* in Northern NJ, to visit the animals. We drove in a brand-new station-wagon which Ky borrowed from his auto-dealership. A cute, young bear came to the car, I fed her cookies through the window; (ignoring the signs stating "DO NOT FEED THE ANIMALS"). Then, another huge bear came running, I quickly closed the windows. The bear was angry, he put his paws on the car, and started rocking. We took off. The next day Ky returned the car with two giant paw-print indentations.

STORY: Before we readied our house for sale, we had the exterior painted. After completion, I emptied the remaining 5gal can into the dumpster. When it was removed, it leaked a thin, trailing white stripe along the road, starting from our house down Blakeslee road. Neighbors complained, thinking that I purposely painted the stripe to show that our house was for sale! Bill Fischer was our realtor.

STORY: The family we sold our home to were Chinese and owned a Chinese restaurant. As we sat at the realtor's office negotiating the price, the buyer mentioned that her son was born on February 22. Knowing that Chinese strongly believed in numerology, I took a napkin and wrote down $222,222. That ended the negotiations, and became the agreed-on price!

STORY: A week after the closing, as per their request, I visited the family to help explain the operation of the thermostats and appliances. When I arrived, I was shocked to see that my 400 square-foot office had been converted to three bed-rooms, a living-room, and a shower. A total of (13) people lived there, and they complained that they were not getting enough hot-water?

We were season ticket holders at the *Oakdale Theater* where we saw great shows, including: Tom Jones, Karen Carpenter, Barbara Streisand, Dion Warwick, Liberace, Whitney Houston, Don Rickles, Neil Sedaka, Frankie Valli, Natalie Cole (we got a refund from her show), Diana Ross, Jerry Vale, Steve Lawrence, and many, many others.

Pilgrim Harbor: In 1987, we purchased a condo at #28B *Pilgrim Harbor*, in Wallingford, CT. This was a beautiful condo overlooking the golf course. Although we never lived there, Sandy did play golf occasionally (while I was looking for lost balls). Helaine and Harold lived here after they married, but only for a short time.

Ridges: We bought a condo at *The Ridges*, which was also at the *Pilgrim Harbor* Golf Course. We had bought it as an investment for our future, so we rented it out, but never lived there.

Lakeridge: On November 1, 1999 we purchased a home at *Lakeridge Resorts,* at *190 Ridge Road,* Torrington, CT. Our home was opposite the street from Sandy's brother *Morris Winkler.* 85% of the residents were New Yorkers, who would drive up on week-ends. It consisted of a group of 460 condos, with 22 tennis courts, a platform tennis court, indoor and outdoor pools, a pond and lake, horse-back riding, and even a ski-lift. We traveled there every Thursday till Monday, as it was only a one and a half hour ride from Wallingford. The houses were very 'hidden' in the woods, making them very rustic. It was loved by those who were used to living in the concrete jungles of New York City.

The only bad part of living there was that it was perpetually dark. The trees covered all the sunlight, and caused mold to grow on the outside walls. We did meet some great friends, *Roy* and *Judy Snyder* whom we see often.

In September 2001, I volunteered to join the Lakeridge Board of Directors; for the next three years. This was the worst experience I have ever had. I flew from Las Vegas to attend monthly Board meetings; what an unappreciative job!

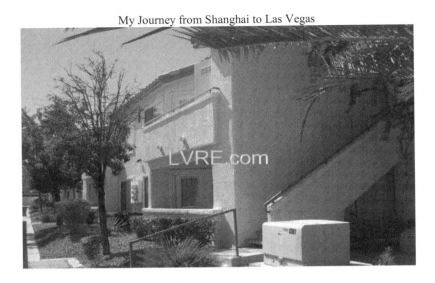

Canyon Willows: While I traveled frequently to the Far East, our kids were now grown up. We had an 'empty nest' and Sandy was left alone. As she loved to gamble, we invested in a condo at the *Canyon Willows* in Las Vegas. We lived on the 2nd floor, where we had to climb a severe fire-escape type stair-case. I hated that climb when we came with groceries and/or water jugs. No, we don't travel frequently to the casinos, and we rarely visited the Strip. I had another thought to moving here. I was going to advertise in a Japanese newspaper to offer a week's stay with unlimited golf. Unfortunately the condo did not allow short-term rentals, thus shattering my plans.

Our friends and family that had come and stayed with us here were: *Sheila Kasten, Morris* (died August 11, 2011) and *Marilynn Winkler, Marvin* (died June 28, 2010) and *Caryl Ashkin, Phyllis Weisberger* (died June 28, 2011), *Iris Goldstein* (died September 22, 1998), *Louise Penta,* and, of course our kids.

I finally had my own bathroom sink. We grew from having one bathroom (shared with Sandy, Helaine, Eric and Dana), to 4 bathrooms with double sinks-WOW what luxury!

184

STORY: On one trip to Las Vegas, our luggage was misplaced enroute. I cheered because the next day a taxi-driver had to climb those steep stairs with our luggage, the tip I gave him was the best investment ever.

STORY: When we finally sold this condo, I also sold our bedroom set to our realtor, for a bargain price of $500. However, two weeks passed and we had not gotten any thanks, or the check? When I called the realtor, I was told her husband had a heart attack going down those steep stairs!

Together with our friends *Lou & Joan Barle*, we traveled to the magnificent Grand Canyon, and beautiful Sedona. To get there, Sandy drove in a rented Cadillac on a treacherous path along a steep cliff; it was a miracle that we didn't fall into the canyon. At an art gallery in Sedona, the girls bought denim jackets with hand-painted Indian warriors for our daughters.

Before we bought our LV home at the Canyon Willow, we had a time-share at the *Jockey Club*. It was a great place on the Strip across from the *Aladdin* (now *Planet Hollywood*), which we owned and used for the next 15 years. On November 21, 1980 we witnessed the MGM casino (now Bally's) catching fire, we could see it from our window. We ultimately 'sold' the time-share to Caryl & Marve, for $1.00.

STORY: *Tom Zappala*, my barber, went to work one morning, when he saw his cat had been run over in front of his house. Knowing how upset his kids would be, he drove to the Animal Pound to get another cat. As he got home with the stray cat, he found his own cat prancing around the house!

Oxford Greens: On October 3, 2005 we moved into *Oxford Greens* at 80 Links Way, Oxford, CT. This is a group of 55+ condos. We're generally here for six months, from May to October. Before moving here, however, I had to make sure that the trees were at least 20' from the house perimeter, to convince Sandy that it would not be dark like it had been at Lakeridge.

This was part of a *Dell Web* community; similar to condos built in and around Las Vegas. These builders however were very difficult to work with. They were so inflexible not allowing any changes. We wanted them not to varnish the stairs going up to the 2nd floor; when we arrived after the closing, the stairs had indeed been varnished!

We live in a Cul-de-sac with (18) other families; what a great group, we meet for cocktails the first Monday of each month; either at the Parklet or at the Ridge Club, depending on the weather. Our closest friends here are *Frank & Terri Sherkus*, *Walter & Bert Weigl*, *Charlie & Arlene Tomer*, and *Chuck & Norma Fleischman*. We have *Marilza* (from Brazil) to take care of our house.

186

When we first moved here, I installed a white lattice fence covering the open area under our deck. (It was identical to a fence the community installed around a water-pump). Upon an inspection, the Oxford Greens Board voted that it did not meet their 'aesthetic guidelines', so I was told to remove it, which I disobligingly did.

STORY: On April 21, 2016, while having dinner with *Sandy* and *Rebecca Sheftel* in New Haven, we met former president Bill Clinton eating at *Pepe's* (world's best pizza).

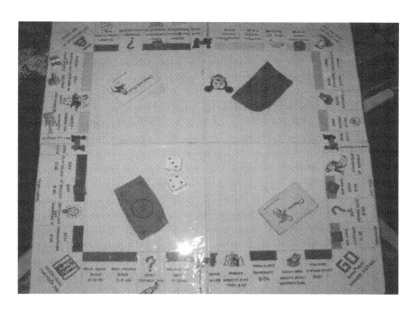

As I was now approaching semi-retirement, I started lots of new hobbies; I molded and painted a ceramic sink in our powder-room; I also created a ceramic Monopoly board (idea copied from Marvin's), which stated the dates of when our kids were born and married, and other major events in Sandy's and my career.

Siena: On August 23, 2000 we went bi-coastal and bought our 3rd home in *Siena* at 10643 Angelo Tenero Ave, Las Vegas, NV, a 55+ age-restricted community. As we thought that our kids would visit us frequently, we bought a large house with four bedrooms; but they rarely come, and never together! Living in three homes became rather difficult, we never knew in which house we left our things, so we had to duplicate everything! We eventually reduced it to two; Las Vegas in the Fall & Winter, Oxford in the Spring & Summer.

What attracted me here was that we overlooked the 8th hole of the beautiful Siena golf-course (but not the casinos). Although I did not play golf at the time, I wanted to be sure that we would retain a beautiful view that would never be obstructed. Also, it had a courtyard, with a running fountain (great Feng Shui), as seen from my office. *Xoshi* takes care of our house twice each week. Nevada became our legal residence (no income tax) after we bought that house.

In contrast to our experience in CT, we were offered 10 pages of upgrades and possible changes; we spent two days making our selections. They even allowed us to eliminate pony-walls opening up the rooms.

As the house was still under construction, we found that the builder had made a mistake and built a 3rd car garage, which we did not want. I subsequently negotiated with the builder to close up the garage door, and built us a 'bonus' room, which became our exercise room. Another mistake was with the front door; we had ordered a leaded, beveled glass door, which they said was no longer available. We liked the door that they had in their model-home, so I insisted to get that door installed, which they finally did.

Being three hours behind the East coast has advantages, (except when we get calls from people at 6:00am who are unaware of the time difference). We have great security here: we're in an armed, guard-gated community (requiring a driver's license to enter and owner's permission), 24/7 patrolled guards by *Securitas*, Rolladen (metal shutters) covering all doors and windows, panic-alarm button (connects directly to the police), remote-locked 10' gate, Ring doorbell, and alarm monitored by *Stanley Security*.

STORY: I had a deposition in New York for a project involving a child's Walker. I stayed at the Plaza Hotel the night before. Eating breakfast, at the adjacent table, was Israel's president *Simon Peres* and his entourage. While I was sitting there, holding this huge box containing the subject Walker, the Israeli Security was eyeing me suspiciously.

Our closest friends here are *Carol & Harold Herzlich* (who used to live only five houses from us in Wallingford; they've been our friends for 50+ years). Our other best friends are *Sheila & Abe Schwartz* (who left Las Vegas moved to Florida, and have returned back to LV); also *Len & Linda Eckhaus* (whom we can see from across the golf-course); *Ira & Helen Rosenmertz* (who is my golf partner); *Mark & Pat Yoseloff* (both of whom worked with me at Coleco); and *Shirley* (died April 22, 2008) and *David Harris*.

189

It was Len who urged me to write this book, which I did start after reading his biography of *"Lessons I've Learned Along the Way"*. They were the first friends we met when we moved here. After the closing, we had to have our landscaping completed within 90 days, so we were driving around looking at nice landscaped yards, that's how we met!

We also became friends with *Dvir* & *Anfisa Bar-Gal* (who also live in Shanghai, are tour guides to the Shanghai Ghetto), living part-time in Las Vegas, and also *Evelyn Wolpert* (who came from Shanghai and appears in a kindergarten picture with me). Friends and family that had come and stayed with us here were: *Caryl, Debbie & Louis, Roy & Judy Snyder, Terri & Frank Sherkus*, Gail & *Art Gronbach*, Sandy's cousins *Larry, Nancy & Matt Kline*, our dog sitter *Kim & John Isberg, David Harris*, my Israeli cousins *Eytan & Marcella, Uri & Revital, Liat & Eretz*, Gail's parents *Ted* (died April 26, 2017) & *Mary Roche*, Harold's parents *Bill* (died April 10, 2014) & *Ann Fischer*, and of course our kids.

We frequently go to the Strip to see shows and performers, some of which included: The Blue-Man Group, Celine Dion, Paul Anka, Engelbert Humperdinck, Elton John, Clint Holmes (jazz singer), Terri Fader (ventriloquist), Billy Joel, David Copperfield (magician), Jerry Lewis (comedian), Gladys Knight, Whitney Houston, the Tenors, Neil Diamond, Cirque-du-Soleil, and America's Got Talent (filming of the TV show).

Feng Shui

For our past several houses, we hired a Master *Feng Shui* to help guide us in its purchase. She helped us choose which house to buy and what interior arrangements we should make. In our Las Vegas home, per her advice, we removed several pony walls, which opened up our living room. What is Feng Shui?

[10] "Feng Shui is the ancient Chinese practice of rules to govern spatial arrangement and orientation in relation to the laws of energy, and effects favorable or unfavorable energy to harmonize individuals with their surroundings."

Suggestions to have good Feng Shui and avoid bad Chi:
☺ Bathroom mirrors should not split down the middle.
☺ Bathrooms should be ventilated, toilet seats down.
☺ Bedroom mirrors should be alongside the bed.
☺ Bedroom picture over bed should be one, not two.
☺ Headboard against a wall, no toilet on other side.
☺ House should always be clean, airy, and uncluttered.
☺ Entrance should have flowing water & fountain/fish.

Our Vacations

Sandy and I have enjoyed many great vacations together, from several cruises to the Caribbean, to Israel, to the Mediterranean, to our Safari in Africa. Here are some of the places and trips we've been to:

72- Cruise to Bermuda & Nassau (with Dick/Camille):
☺ The cruise and sights were wonderful, but Sandy became sea-sick on the boat when it became bumpy; you would see her sitting (alone) on a deck-chair on the ship's bow. [we cruised together again in '74 and '78].

78- Trip>Lisbon Algarve, Portugal (Caryl/Marve/Phyllis/Bill)
Saw: Lisbon's Caravel monument, Algarve beaches.
☺ Our first trip we took together with the 3 sisters.

79- Trip to Santa Domingo (Caryl/Marve/Phyllis/Bill/Morris):
☺ The movie '*Brothers in Blood*' was being filmed at our hotel featuring Bo Svenson, Martin Balsam (looks like Bill Weisberger); extras were: Sandy, Helaine, Phyllis, Caryl, Diane, Bill and Debbie, became featured actors.

192

80- Trip to Israel (with Caryl/Marve/Phyllis/Bill):
   To: Jerusalem, TelAviv, Haifa, Netanya, Masada, Caesarea
   Saw: Western Wall, Yad Vashem, Dome-Rock, Stations.

86- Trip to Hong Kong, China (with Helaine/Eric/Dana).

87- Trip to Rome:
   Saw: Coliseum, Forum, St Peter's, Sistine, Catacombs.

92- Trip to London (with Dana):
   Saw: Westminster, Tower of London, Buckingham.

93- Trip to Rome, Vatican & Israel (with Dana):
   ☺ On our return flight, we landed in Rome (via El Al).
   At the airport coming from Israel, we were escorted to
   the gate by two tanks- very SCARY.
   Saw: Chagall windows, Hadassah Hospital.

94-Trip to HongKong, Guangzhou, Shekow, China (Caryl/Marve)
   ☺ I sponsored this trip for our very appreciative sister
   and brother Caryl & Marve, we had a great trip together.

95- Trip to Hawaii, Macao, Hong Kong & China (business):
   Saw: Diamond Head (climbed to top of volcano).

96- Trip to Israel:
   ☺ We spent lots of time with my 1st cousins *Eytan,*
   Marcella, Uri, Revital their kids, my aunt and uncle
   Yitzhak and Ilse Cohen. **SHALOM**

97- Trip to Disney World (with Eric/Gail/kids):

97- Trip to Hong Kong, China, Singapore, Tokyo (Eric/Dana)
   Saw: Tokyo Disney Land, Bullet train.

98- Trip to Israel: (just us).

99- Trip to Shanghai, Beijing, Guangzhou, Macau, China:
Saw: My Shanghai home, Great Wall, Forbidden City.
☺ We stayed at the 23rd floor of the *Shangri-La* hotel in Pudong, Shanghai. Because of an Economic Conference at the Convention Center across the street, we were not allowed to open the drapes to view the 50th anniversary celebration of the Chinese Revolution. Police searched with binoculars to ensure our drapes were always closed.

01- Trip to Israel (with Helaine/Harold/kids):

02- Trip to Disney World (with Eric/Gail/kids):

03- Trip to Disney Institute:
☺ An educational and fun trip. We took lessons in golf, animation, film-making, cartoons, cooking & gardening.

04- Trip to Disney World (with Eric/Gail/kids):

05- Oceanic cruise to Bermuda & Nassau (Dick/Camille):

05- Trip to San Francisco (with Caryl/Marvin):
Saw:Sequaia's, cable car, Chinatown, Fisherman's Wharf.
☺ Was a great trip, Marvin and I eating Dungeness crab, and Caryl throwing up on the Golden Gate Bridge.

06- Trip to Maui, Hawaii (Helaine/Harold/Eric/Gail/kids):
☺ We had a party for Ari celebrating his Bar Mitzvah the whole family went horse-back riding, but Zach's horse laid down and refused to budge. Jordan hated seeing the roasted pig at the luau. **MAHALO**
☺ We all went SNUBA diving (with tethered Scuba gear) I was unable to stick my head under water; had to give up

07- Railroad trip to Alaska (with Ari/Jordan):
Saw: glaciers, orcas, whales, seals & reindeer.

194

08- Trip>Atlantis, Paradise Isl. (Caryl/Marve/Dana/Angela):
☺ Best part was Sandy, PJ, I swimming with Dolphins.

09- Trip to Buffalo and Niagara, Canada (with Caryl/Marve):
Saw: Anchor Buffalo Wings, Niagara Falls, Maid-of-Mist

11- River cruise on the Danube (with Roy/Judy):
To: Budapest, Slovakia, Vienna, Germany, Prague.
Saw: Theresienstad, Mathausen, Riga Concentration Camps

11- Carnival cruise to the Caribbean (with Caryl/Diane):
To: St Kitts, St Lucas, St Maarten, West Indies.

12- Oceanic cruise along the Baltic (with Mark/Pat):
To: Riga, Berlin, Helsinki, Copenhagen, Sweden, Russia.
Saw: Berlin Wall, Holocaust Museum, Hermitage, Church of Spilled Blood in St Petersburg.
☺ In Germany, *Mark* and *Pat Yoseloff* either lost, or had their passports stolen. They had to obtain replacements at the U.S. Consulate in Denmark.

13- Trip to San Diego & Tijuana, Mexico (with Norm):
Saw: Model Train Museum (Balboa Park), Oak Furniture.

13- Oceanic cruise along the Mediterranean:
To: Barcelona, Nice, Marseille, Cannes, Monte Carlo, Naples, Florence, Vienna.
Saw: Gaudi, Chagall paintings, David, Pompeii, Pisa, St.Stevens cathedral, Schönbrunn castle, Spanish Riding.
☺ While waiting for a bus in Marseille for our return to the ship. I saw someone who looked familiar. Indeed he was, he turned out to be *Jerry Fogel,* our neighbor with whom I frequently played golf at Oxford Greens.

14- Oceanic cruise to Israel & Mediterranean (Mark/Pat):
To: Istanbul, Ephesus, Cinque, Athens, Rhodes, Israel.
Saw:Blue Mosque, Grand Bazaar, Acropolis, Bahai.

☺ While in Istanbul I was talked into buying a 5'x8' hand-sewn silk carpet. The asking price was US$3,200, (which sounded ridiculous), I then negotiated it down to $800 (which seemed like I was buying junk); but after a long and difficult fight, I finally got my deposit back.

14- Trip to Disney World (with Eric/Gail/parents/kids):

15- Princess Cruise along West Coast to Vancouver, Victoria.
Saw: magnificent *Buchart* Gardens.

15- Trip to Atlantis (with Dana/Angela/Helaine/Harold/kids):
☺ Best part was Helaine and I swimming with the seals.

17- Safari to Kenya, Tanzania, Africa:
Saw: *Maasai* warriors jumping (to determine who could jump the highest); the 'Great Migration' thousands of zebra and wildebeest in Serengeti; petted baby orphaned Elephants at the *David Sheldrick* Trust; a lion's kill of a zebra; and a cheetah's kill of a gazelle.
STORY: We brought boxes of crayons, scissor, pencils, and coloring books to pass out to the Maasai children (Mara village in Kenya), enough for (15) kids. But, (63) kids lined up, so we had a give each only one crayon.

STORY: After we returned from a Safari ride, I went to take a nap. Sandy suddenly screamed when a huge baboon entered our room through the balcony door. The baboon sat on the desk and took a bag of Sandy's newly purchased hats, and a package of bubble-gum. She surrendered the hats (nothing to eat), but passed the gum out to her baboon family.

My Business trips where to:
Hanover, Zurich, Tijuana, Montreal, Toronto.
Beijing/Guangzhou, Shanghai, Shenzhen, Shekou, Ningbo, Macao, HK, Taipei, Tokyo, Osaka, Kuala Lumpur, Seoul, Manila, Bangkok

Part 6

Reiner Associates

(1988 - 2015)

A New Career

After 19 years, I was laid off from Coleco. The layoff, and the bankruptcy the following month, cancelling my seven months of severance, was a huge shock to me; my paychecks stopped, my insurance stopped, my leased car stopped! I wanted to buy the furniture that was in my office; even for that Coleco charged me $2,000! I immediately sent out hundreds of resumes, but no responses were received. **What to do NEXT?**

In June 1988, I started *REINER Associates, Inc.* I got my first assignment with *Tomy*, Japan, to help with their Quality Assurance. I traveled to Japan, Hong Kong, Taiwan, and Thailand assisting with their QA and QC.

While enroute, traveling from JFK to TOK, I realized that I needed a logo for my business card, a MUST in Japan. I took the United emergency card from the seat jacket; turned the United logo around, and that became my 'REINER' logo:

 REINER ASSOCIATES INC
ENGINEERING & MANUFACTURING CONSULTANTS

At first, life was very scary. Since I was twelve I had never been without a job. Although all the kids were out of college, I still had two homes with mortgages. My mother gave me $20K; *Nate & Iris* came with a check (which I did not accept). I had received $109K from my Coleco contributed Pension Plan, but thankfully I never needed to touch it. Although they pushed for me to continue with this plan, I said that I wanted the cash to be invested! **YAA...**

Fortunately, when Coleco closed its doors, there were many engineers and marketing people who left for companies throughout the industry. I knew someone at virtually every toy company. This allowed me the opportunity to make the necessary introductions to get some consulting opportunities. Almost immediately I got my first job with McDonalds.

I also received great assignments from the following:
Paul Meyer- Superior, Playnet, InterAct, ShuffleMast, UDeck
Jim Boudreau- Naki, A.T.Cross, Miacomet, Genesis.
Brian Clarke- Toy Biz, Leather, Tragar Oil.
Chuck Bookstaver- Mattel, Roadmaster, Flexible Flyer.
Bob Andrews- Hedstrom, BD+A.
Ty Boukley- Intex, Marchon, Typhoon.
Herb Hewitt- Tomy USA,
John Driska- Remco, Kiddesign.

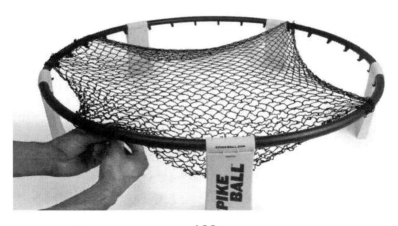

198

In 1979, shortly after I got started, I got a job from *Tomy USA*, a newly formed group to create products for Tomy, led by *Phil Jackson*. One of these projects was '*Spike Ball*', usually played on a beach or lawn. The game consists of a ball and trampoline; with rules similar to Volleyball. I did the design and manufacturing; Tomy did fairly well, but it was more a sport than a toy. As the inventor never patented the product, many years later it became a huge success after it was reintroduced (by different people) on 'Shark Tank'. Too bad I was not still involved!

My auto license(s) are **TOY MKR**.

To get myself known during the 1989 Toy Fair, I created and conducted a seminar called '*Toy Tech*'. I had several guest speakers talk about Toy Safety, Manufacturing, and Quality Assurance. This helped me get started, and led to a successful consulting career; the following were my staff:

Reiner Associates, Inc (U.S.):

Address:	21 Blakeslee Road, Wallingford, CT
Incorporated:	July 1, 1988
Bert Reiner	President and CEO
Frank Mercurio	Engineering Director
Bob Amici	Engineering Manager
Alberta Fiore	Administrator and Bookkeeper

Reiner Associates, Ltd (H.K.):

Address:	58 Chuen Ping St. Kwai Chung, HK
Incorporated:	February 7, 1991
Bert Reiner:	Managing Director
Chi Cheong Lo:	Engineering Manager
Ivy Cheung:	Administrator and Office Manager
William Mo:	QC Engineer and Inspector

The following is a summary of what we did for some of my major clients:

Mattel

During my first Toy Fair after my lay-off, I met with several Mattel executives and was given a huge opportunity to design and manufacture a line of blow-molded outdoor toys. My engineer *Frank Mercurio* had the unique knowledge of designing blow-molded stuff. We then created and manufactured a line of Mickey, Minnie, Donald, and Pluto ride-ons, as well as other outdoor blow-molded products. These were molded and assembled at *Mac Plastics*, in Pittsburgh. This business became huge; in 1990 my gross was over $4 million. My concern was, what would I do if they cancelled any of their orders? (I did include in my contract that of cancellation, I would get a rebate of cost-plus 15%)

STORY: One product did get cancelled, it was for their order of *Pluto Rockers*. Mattel paid me for all the unshipped product; so I kept the left-over's in the vendor's warehouse. About a year later, Mattel advised that they had a customer. I then found out that they had already been ground up and was forced to reimburse Mattel.

Sanitoy

We developed and manufactured several infant items for *Sanitoy*. Included were the *Time-Out-Timer* (patent #5,872,746), *Tooth-Timer* (a positive timer to set for 2 minute timing while brushing a kid's teeth, the idea was conceived by Helaine), also *Einstein* and *Talking Giraffe*.

STORY: The Tooth-Timer was a great success. however, the 40' container in the shipment capsized, and disappeared at sea.

STORY: As my China manufacturing and QC started to grow, I set up an Engineering office and QC staff in Hong Kong, headed by my Engineer *C.C. Lo,* Administrator *Ivy Cheung* and Inspector *William Mo*. At first, I had my inspectors sleep and eat at my vendor's dormitories, but that proved to be a conflict of interest, so I rented an apartment and signed a two-year lease. Less than a month after I signed the lease, I got a bill for some plumbing for the new apartment; my inspector had removed the new toilet and replaced it with a 'hole in the floor' Chinese toilet.

During 1995, Helaine and I also developed a hand-held device to track mothers to nurse, feed, and diaper their infant. We patented this idea, and on November 25, 1997 we received patent #5,691,932 "CARE GIVER DATA COLLECTION & REMINDER SYSTEM". We sold a non-exclusive license of our idea to Sanitoy; who placed an order for 25K units with REINER Associates, for the design and production.

STORY: During one of my (many) trips, from Hong Kong to China, my passport was stolen, along with my return ticket, drivers license, and credit cards. First I went to a Police station in China to report the crime, then went to the American Embassy in Guangzhou to get a new passport. Since I had no ID to prove who I was, or that I was indeed American, the Consul General would not agree to give me one. I asked him where he planned to spend his Christmas? He replied "with his family"; so I told him "... *I will plan to join you at your home for the holidays, as you won't allow me to get to mine*". Then, together with Sandy's help faxing over my Naturalization docs; I was off the hook (sort of). I could not use my photo (a Polaroid taken from a kiosk), so I was given a 'temporary' passport good for only 7 days; but, enough to get me home for the holidays.

In the early days of working in China (the 70s), it was very difficult getting in and out:

a) An entry visa might take two days to get.
b) All jewelry, watches, phones had to be registered upon entry into China, and checked again on departure.
c) All video cameras were looked at to check for pornography and/or propaganda.
d) Service in restaurants was terrible, (waiters threw dishes).
e) Waiters and chauffeurs (considered equals) would eat at the table with you, and you were required to pay for them.
f) If your hotel room had two beds, a stranger might be required to share the room.

Precise

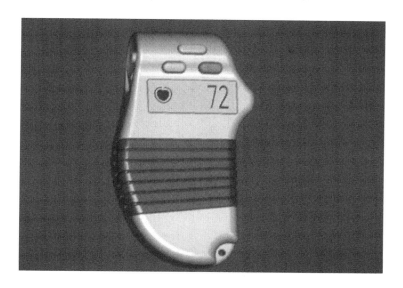

An attendee of my *Toy Tech* seminar was *Opher Pail*, of *Precise International*, of Orangeburg, NY. This was a Swiss company licensed to make and sell the Swiss Army knife in the U.S. We developed and manufactured several Pedometers (PED #1+3), plus models with added features like Golf (PED #4), Pulse Reading (PED #5+9), Safety Light (PED #7), Thermometer (PED #8), Alarm (PED #10), Talking (PED #11), and a Stop-Watch. We grossed over $400K between 1993-98. These units were designed in my office in the U.S., and manufactured in China and Taiwan. The business suddenly stopped when Opher was arrested for mismanagement of Precise funds, issuance of patents under his name, and other malfeasance.

STORY: The engineering work which we did in the U.S., was with the *AutoCAD* software. I had gotten the software from Coleco, not knowing that it was illegally obtained from the streets of Hong Kong. When we got caught, the company Autodesk advised us to either pay $3,500 for the legal software, or they would turn us into the FBI; I chose the former.

Aura

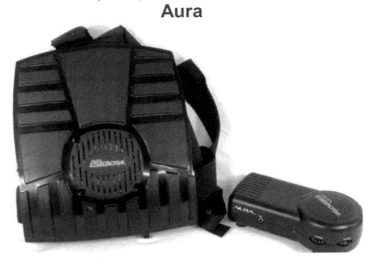

During the 1994 *CES show* held in Las Vegas, I located a company *Aura Systems,* of El Segundo, CA who were about to release the *Interactor*; a vest with a sound transducer that translated lo-frequency sounds into vibrations. To describe: If you played a boxing video, you would actually 'FEEL' getting hit.

After the show, I met with *Harry Kurtzman*, their CEO, at the lobby of the *Waldorf Astoria*, to make my 'pitch'. I proposed that I prepare a product quote, for a $5,000 retainer; he agreed and I got the job!

Aura had placed a total of 350,000 units, but sales did not do well, as the product proved to be too expensive ($150 retail). Eventually, I was asked to stop production and cancel all their outstanding orders. There were seven vendors (including me) that were owed a total of US $4.5 million. Aura had run out of money, how will my vendors get paid? Harry and I traveled to Hong Kong to meet with each vendor (and their lawyers) to convince them to accept unregistered shares of Aura stock, which they had to hold for a minimum of 90 days, after which time they could sell their stocks. The scam worked, all vendors got paid!

Triax

One day, I got a visit from *Roger Kolsky* of Albany, NY who had an idea he wanted us to develop. I suggested that they return with $5,000 for us to get started. Their idea was a device on which you could move your finger on a flat pad, similar to what is now used in lieu of a mouse, on almost all laptop computers. They returned four weeks later with a check! We subsequently developed and manufactured for *Triax Technologies* a line of video controllers for use with Nintendo, Sega and PC games. During 1993-95 my gross sales with them was almost $500,000.

Unfortunately all did not go well; in 1995 Triax got a major investor who in return, received 60% of the Triax stock, and subsequently closed their doors. With the help of *Jim Boudreau*, they then sold the company's assets to a competitor *Naki Controllers*, who continued to place more orders with me. However, they too eventually filed for bankruptcy, and I then endured a total loss of $93,000. At the next CES, they were back in business, under a different name.

Fridays

During the 1994 Toy Fair, I met *Anne Schrader* and *Deb Baker* (originally from Coleco). They were attempting to introduce a line of little girl's dress-up clothing. Anne did the designing, Deb did the sales, and I did the manufacturing. They sold to all the major chains, including Sam's Club, BJ's, Target, Wal-Mart, K-Mart and Sears. One of the sales to Sam's Club was for 18 container's of Dress-up trunks. For the four years I grossed over $350,000; until they sold the co.

Researching for this book, I found the following FAX dated July 2, 1995, which Sandy wrote when she accompanied me on one of my business trips:

Mon: Today we spent the day touring Honolulu.

Tue: This morning we left Hawaii (regretfully) having a nice smooth flight to Tokyo, then on to Hong Kong. We are staying at the Royal Garden Hotel, in a Jr Suite room #606, (wow, Bert's life is not too shabby)! We each had a heaping bowl of Won Ton soup, then to bed at 1:00am.

Wed: I slept well (but only till 3:00am), we're leaving for Macao and China on the 7:30am ferry. We went with two women from Ringling Circus, they're very nice. It was really rough going, we went by hydrofoil (skimming over the water) which was very bumpy, fortunately I took Dramamine. Before and after the ride you have to go through Immigration and Customs. It's really very difficult if you do this frequently, I don't know how Bert does it? We went to the Carice (Jimmy Lee) factory.

We got back that evening, had dinner with Jimmy (He looks good as he had a 6-way bypass only two months ago). Dinner was wonderful, I had veal; was nice not to have Chinese again! I had no problem falling asleep, but woke again at 3:00am.

Thu: We met Ivy (Bert's assistant), who was to take me into China, then met Delphine (from Bob's factory) after I got another visa, but had to wait because the office doesn't open till 9:00am. Then we went by train, to meet Bert and Deb at the TriS factory, what a *shlep*. This day was devoted to Friday's (Dress-up products). Next we went to the (doll) Shoe factory, Bert rejected all their production; the owner was a nice guy, but the shoes were crappy, it's great to watch Bert in action; he's really wonderful with people, even when he's giving hell.

Then on to Friday's main factory, run by Tallman (he's about 6'0"), that was a pleasure, as he does nice quality. His driver then drove us directly back to Hong Kong (still had to go through Immigration and Customs, but that was much easier). Had dinner with Tallman (I've been having a problem as we've been going to the best Chinese Seafood restaurants; I told him I was a vegetarian, that the only seafood I eat is lobster; so that's what he ordered, a gigantic 6# lobster .

Fri: Today I stayed in Hong Kong shopping, shopping and more shopping; Deb took me around, she's a real doll. For dinner, we were with James Wong (HonorTone) at the Holiday Inn; I ordered my favorite, Sweet & Sour pork.

Sat: After visiting another sub-contractor for Ringling this morning; Bert made a sales-presentation of the Friday's line to Kmart of Australia. I was so proud and impressed with him.

For lunch we had Won Ton at the Nanking Noodle shop. This afternoon, more shopping. For dinner, we went to Gaddi's (one of the world's top 10 restaurants) with Bob and Debbie Simmons. It was the nicest evening we've spent so far. They are wonderful (Bert had actually introduced them to each other), I love them both. Since we had our anniversary just two weeks ago, they had a cake for us, played the Anniversary Waltz, and gave us a beautiful Baccarat vase. I hope we will have enough time to see them again before we leave.

Sun: Today we did more shopping (for glasses, lot's cheaper than from my cousin Larry). Tonight we were with Alan Cheng (Silvine); it was nice to have seen him again. He and Stella were in Las Vegas last month, together with their two kids. He stayed at Caesar's; had a 4 bedroom suite with it's own pool. His friend lost $200K (Alan didn't say whether he won or lost). Helaine: We just called you guys, was disappointed not to find you at home. We don't expect Eric, Gail, Dana or Angela at home today, so we won't try. I spoke with Barbra the other day, she said that Nate may go back into Intensive Care, I hope he has the stamina to live through all of this, I wonder how much longer he can take?

Mon: Bert is still sleeping, it's only 4:30am. We haven't bought any clothes here this trip, things are no longer inexpensive (except for eyeglasses and food). Eric and Gail: Happy Anniversary, will try to call you later. Just got back from a breakfast meeting with Simon Wong (he used to work for Bert at Ideal).

Called Trudy, we were happy that Dana and Angela visited her at Daughters of Miriam; she likes it there! Tonight we're having dinner with Vincent Li (Precise) and his wife. Tomorrow we're off for home! *We love you all, Mom*

Ringling Bros

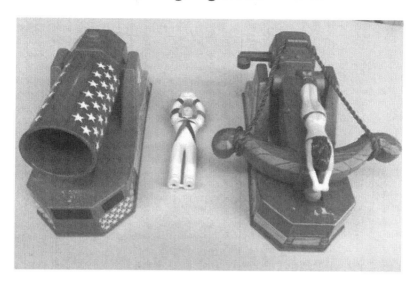

In 1995 I pursued an interesting job with the *Kenneth Feld Co* in Washington, DC., who own the *Ringling Brothers Circus*. My team, which consisted of *Frank Mercurio, Bob Amici* and *C.C. Lo* (my engineer in Hong Kong), developed several novelty toys which were sold at the Circus. Some of those items were the Cannon (see above), the Globe of Death, Disney pens, etc. I had grossed $400K with Ringling over the next four years.

STORY: During one of the trips via train back to my Hong Kong hotel, I felt something biting my leg. I looked down and saw this woman standing next to me, carrying several live chickens. She had them in a bag with holes, where they peeked out and proceeded to peck at my leg.

STORY: On the first trip with the whole family, we were having an elaborate dinner at *Kenneth Ting*'s factory *Kader* in Shekow, China. Dana had to go to the bathroom. He returned a few minutes later, shaking with an ashen face, telling us there was no toilet, only a hole in the floor!

In 1998 I started consulting and designing work for *Marc Segan* of the *M.H. Segan Co.*, on several projects for *Mr. Christmas*, of New York. This project consisted of designing the '*Santa's Ski Slope*'. Instead of a train traveling around a Christmas tree, it had a ski-slope with several figures, riding up and down and around the tree. I also assisted with the QA of several framed 3D Animatronic designs: Tweety & Sylvester, Bugs Bunny & Elmer, and Micky Mouse & Steamboat Willie.

STORY: I love Won Ton soup. On one of the business trips that I went with Sandy and the boys; we wanted to eat at the *Nanking Noodle Shop*, but we never had the chance. Finally, on our last day in Hong Kong, I sent Eric across the street to get some Won Ton soup for us to eat before our departure. When Eric finally arrived, the limo was already waiting and it was time to depart for the airport. Enroute, we found the soup leaking all over the Mercedes' limo floor. Upon arrival at the airport, we gave the driver a smile, a big tip, and we hurried of.

210

Tara

The *Tara Toy Corp*, located in Hauppauge, NY, made children's vinyl-covered carrying cases, mostly for *Barbie*. My project was a pull-along-carrier to hold (100) Hot-Wheel cars; it became one of my most difficult projects as it required a big, difficult and expensive mold. My engineer *Frank Mercurio* did a fine job on the engineering, however it required a lot of changes to the molds.

Tara's principal *Don Pearlman* sued me (for my liaison charges), I prevailed, but with an expensive legal bill.

Another domestic manufacturing client, was the *Trager Oil Company*, of Wantagh, NY, which was an oil company primarily involved in delivering heating oil to consumers. The oil would be pumped into steel tanks housed in people's basements or buried outdoors. Recent laws, however, prohibited the use of in-ground tanks, so they now needed to be stored above ground. For them, I designed a huge polyethylene, roto-molded housing to cover the oil-tanks above ground, which was more pleasing than the exposed steel tanks. These housings were manufactured in the U.S., in upstate NY.

A.T. Cross

In 1997 I was introduced to *A.T.Cross* (the domestic pen company) by *Jim Boudreau,* to develop the '*CrossPad*': an electronic notepad with a special pen which contained a radio transmitter which told the pad what is being written. The software was supplied by *IBM*, and the electronics was developed by *FinePoint Electronics*, of Mesa, AZ). It was manufactured by my old friend *James Wong* from *HonorTone*, in Donguan, China. I grossed $1.3million in the two years that I worked with Cross. Unfortunately the product was not well received and was eventually discontinued.

STORY: On one of my business trips to China, I deviated and spent three days in Shanghai reminiscing my youth. While walking along the *Bund* (famous boardwalk along the Wangpoa river), I recognized a building I thought I

212

remembered as being the *Shanghai Club* where my parents belonged and where I learned to swim. What I remembered from my youth, was a guy always polishing the brass doors. These doors were now painted black. I proceeded to scratch the door's surface with my fingernail, and surprisingly, it was the same brass doors, now covered with 40 years of dirt.

After the Cross project, I continued to work with *FinePoint*, then followed later with *Mutoh* (a Japanese company) to make flexible Mylar PCB boards.

STORY: After each trip I would bring knock-off watches. Although illegal to bring into the U.S., I would manage to smuggle a few Rolex, Movado, Cartier, and/or Patek Philippe. I brought one of these watches to a friend who used to wear the real Rolex. As a joke, he once threw one of these fake watches out his car window, shocking his friends who thought it was his real one.

STORY: On a 'scary' flight to Hong Kong, we stopped first in Anchorage, Alaska. I was sitting in First Class, in the first row, on the right side, at the nose of a 747. As the plane was descending, I looked out to only see WATER, I was sure we were going to crash. Although I did not hear any warnings, I proceeded to the BRACE position. Then, the plane took a sharp turn to the left, and there was the runway!

STORY: On a trip to Bangkok, it was suggested that I explore buying latex rubber gloves that were in extreme short supply. They were used extensively by doctors, nurses, EMT, firemen, etc. So, I visited a condom manufacturer, who quoted gloves at 7.2cents, in container lots, but, I chickened out (was not my expertise). I was good that I did, as the prices dropped severely when Nitrile gloves were introduced.

At midnight, on July 1, 1997, Hong Kong was reverted back to China, after 99 years of British sovereignty.

213

Hedstrom

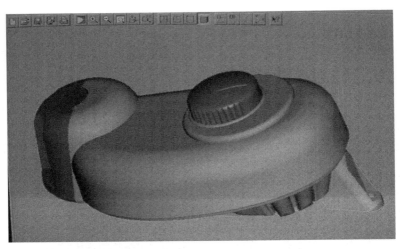

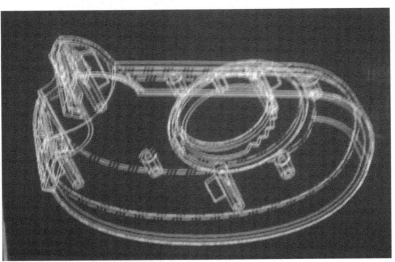

This is a company that was largely into children's sports equipment; i.e. slides, swings, pool accessories, etc. We designed and manufactured a line of sound devices to be added to their products: i.e. Zoom (to add sound to a Slide), also SkeeBall, Rocker, RideOn, ShootOut, and Basketball. (The above picture is a 3D drawing of ZOOM which we created via our ProE Engineering program).

Furniture West:

Work with this client is very different, I consult primarily on the SAFETY of their juvenile furniture for *Oak Furniture West*, located in Tijuana, Mexico. I test their children's dressers and bunk-beds for compliance to ASTM standards. I am an active member of the American Society for Testing and Materials. For their dressers, we check to make sure that they don't tip-over with a 50# weight applied to each drawer (simulating a child standing on the drawer to reach for something). As an Expert Witness, I was involved in several cases where a child was killed from a tip-over. The most notable dresser cases were manufactured by IKEA. I testified against them where four kids were killed.

What do I do with the dressers and bunk-beds after I'm done with the testing? I give them away to friends and relatives (only those that were tested SAFE). In the ten years that I've worked with them doing QA and Safety consulting, I had made several trips to tour and inspect their factories in Mexico. I found them to be well equipped, and very impressive(compared to Chinese factories). After each tour, I was treated to a restaurant featuring deep-fried lobster, **WOW**

215

Miacomet

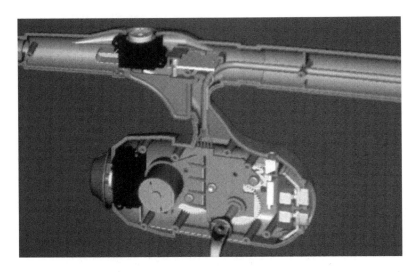

Miacomet was a small video-game software company started by *Dennis Kozlowski*, CEO of Tyco [Tyco became ADT]. (Dennis was later imprisoned for corruption while serving at Tyco. He was caught in a scam where he would buy expensive paintings, with Tyco funds, have them shipped to his home in NY, and then ship the empty crates to their headquarters in NH, thus avoiding to pay NY sales tax. He eventually got caught and spent 6 years in prison.

We developed an electronic fishing-rod & reel for use with fishing software developed by a guy who lived on *Nantucket Island*, neighboring Koslowski's Summer home. Upon completion of that project, we also worked on a pool [billiard] game; but both projects were halted when Dennis faced jail.

QUOTE: "A good speech should be like a woman's skirt; long enough to cover the ass, and short enough to create interest". *Winston Churchil.*

TriSource

In 2009, I started work with *Ed Hyland* of *TriSource*, located in Shelton, CT, he was my favorite client. He was a nice guy, very creative engineer, but not good at Sales. We worked together for many years, but the work was not very lucrative. We worked together developing and manufacturing LED street-Lamps, power-supplies, in-store phone-demos, and multi-iPad chargers. Ed ran out of finances, closed his shop, and moved onto his boat in Florida. He sold his business to *ReadyDock*, in Hartford, CT.

STORY: On one of my business trips with Sandy, as we were passing thru China Immigration returning to Hong Kong, an agent found an irregularity with her visa stamp; This was not her fault, the immigration officer had stamped the wrong visa upon our entry. They whisked Sandy away (leaving her stranded on the China side). I had already passed viewing her from the Hong Kong side. This was scary!

STORY: On one of our earlier trips, I was traveling with one of my vendors K.W. Lee, who was panicking when he could not find his cheap calculator (it would have cost him a fortune if he had inadvertently left it in China).

217

Hartz Mountain

This is the *Hartz Mountain Company*, of Secaucus, NJ., makers of dog, cat, bird and small animal medications, shampoos, treats, and toys. I consulted for them on the safety and durability of their dog and cat toy lines. These were not easy projects to do. How do I translate what I've learned about children's safety, to a 'Fetch and Tug' dog's toy? The answer is lots of patience, and playing with dogs!

This is the letter I wrote in lieu of end-of year gifts:

"This is the time of year when I make plans for holiday gifts for my most valued clients. I've decided to take the funds that I had set aside for this purpose, and donate them in the names of our clients to CHILDREN INTERNATIONAL, a worthwhile effort for underprivileged children. In these times of relative affluence, we often forget about those less fortunate and still suffering. So, this year, I feel that a donation would be of better use, and I trust that you will take some joy knowing that someone homeless may celebrate this holiday season"
Bert Reiner

Genesis

Jim Boudreau was a good friend who got me several business opportunities with *Naki*, *A.T.Cross*, and *Miacomet*; then started his own company *Genesis Inc.* (also known as *Nano Shoppes*). For the latter, I manufactured for him a line of pen holders, cables and tethers.

However, he was not a good business man, always running short of money (but he always did pay what he owed me, though frequently three months late). Eventually he got in trouble, and sold his company to *CFT Shops*. To make sure I wouldn't get burnt again, I began demanding prepayment on all their orders.

QUOTE: "Genius is one percent inspiration, and 99% perspiration". *Tomas Edison*

QUOTE: "People ask you for criticism, but they really only want praise". *William S. Maugham*

ShuffleMaster

ShuffleMaster was a company located in the heart of Las Vegas, making a line of card shufflers used in almost every casino throughout the world (later sold to *Bally's* then *Scientific Games*). In 2004 I was hired by *Mark Yoseloff* (CEO) and *Paul Meyer* COO), both of whom I used to work with at different times during my stay at Coleco. .

I was contracted to review their in-house QC and Service, for their line of casino games. Which included card shufflers, made in Las Vegas, Easy Chipper for dealing chips for Roulette, made in Austria, Rapid Games, combining live dealers with electronic wagering, made in Australia; TableMaster a five-person fully-electronic blackjack game, made in Chicago; and 3Card Poker table games. I oversaw and audited their QA and QC, helped get UL and FCC approvals, and audited facilities in Las Vegas, Chicago, China and Salzburg.

STORY: As part of my audit, I was at a Shuffler installation at *Mandalay Bay* casino, at 6:00am one morning. It was interesting to note that's the time when slot machines are installed, floors cleaned and vacuumed, game table cloth replaced, etc.

While engaged in the above, I also designed and manufactured 3-Card and 4-Card hand-held games which were passed out during Shuffle Master tournaments.

We also designed, but did not manufacture, a low cost card-shuffler for home use, but Shuffle Master decided not to proceed with marketing it. These products were designed by me, together with my engineer, *C.C. Lo*, in Hong Kong.

221

Upper Deck

Upper Deck of Carlsbad, CA, is a company which makes traditional trading cards, sports collectibles and memorabilia. In the past, they mostly handled products for older kids and adults, so they did not find it necessary to engage anyone to review the children's safety aspects of these projects.

As they started to introduce some products for younger children, I was engaged to review the safety, and compliance to the ASTM Standard of their toy lines. I reviewed Hello Kitty toys, Basketball games, Slinger Star Wars, and other products

QUOTE: "One's hardest task is not to do what is right, but to know what is right. *Lyndon B.Johson*

Part 7

Retirement

(2016 - ?)

My Retirement

My retirement did not happen all at once; I was in semi-retirement for several years doing Expert Witness work for lawyers and consulting to the Juvenile products industries. Over time I gave that up.

Sandy had spent years trying to keep my clothes in style; laying out the clothes that I needed to wear like my mother used to do. However, after I retired I no longer needed any suits or dress shirts. Now I only wear shorts, and polo shirts with an array of colors dazzling to the eye.

Since retiring, we've ended up on a whole new sucker list; we get mail, emails, and telephone calls from:

☺ IRS that I immediately pay my outstanding taxes,
☺ Attend seminars on how to avoid taxes,
☺ Won the lottery, pay only a small handling charge,
☺ Send $ to retrieve our grand-son from prison,
☺ Social Security # been suspended, needs to update,
☺ Phishing,
☺ Microsoft or Apple to repair my computer.
☺ Charity relief for hurricane victims, etc.
What's the next SCAM?

I read a lot, but no paper books. I read only on *Kindle* in my *iPhone* or *iPad*, in which I have already 300+ books. For security, Sandy's and my credit are frozen, and I also subscribe to *Life-Lock*. On-line I buy only from *Amazon* (prime). I have a reverse-mortgage on our Las Vegas home, were I get about $2,000/month.

Some of the worst investment decisions are made during difficult times, when investors bail out of equities after periods of market slumps. I believe in riding-thru any 'stock crashes', and hold onto my investments.

Sandy and I have been enrolled in the *"Health & Retirement Study"* sponsored by the National Institute on Aging, for 10+ years. We get interviewed about our health, retirement, etc. each year.

This is what Helaine wrote her mom on Mother's day:

FAMILY: You have always regarded your family--immediate and extended, as the most important value and gift in your life. You modeled that, and I see myself acting in similar ways—*thank you* .

HARDWORK: It's no surprise that I did a lot growing up to help with my brothers when Dad would travel. You often depended on me, as a result, I too am hardworking and a successful mom—*thank you.*

STYLE: You have style, and I realize so do I! People have often complemented me on my unique style – *thank you.*

MARRIAGE: Watching you and Dad, and your advise, has helped Harold and me cement and improve our relationship—*thank you.*

Expert Witnessing

During my last few years that I had been semi-retired, I was doing Expert Witness work for the legal community. I was retained by both Defense (40%) and Plaintiff (60%) attorneys. I am an active member of ASTM Safety committees on Playgrounds, Carriages, Strollers, Cribs, Swings, Dressers, Toys, Swimming Pools, and Bunk-beds. Some of my typical cases are summarized below:

Grasseth v Baby Trend (Plaintiff):
The product involved was a **PLAY-YARD**: a 10 month old infant, while sleeping in the Play-Yard, was found with her neck entrapped in the collapsed Rail. I testified that this product was unsafe as designed.

Tetlow v Hasbro (Plaintiff):
The product involved was a toy **WORK-BENCH**: a 19 month old infant was playing with the subject toy, when she consumed a toy plastic Nail, causing asphyxiation and her subsequent death. I testified this toy was unsafe as designed. Subsequent to this case, I persuaded the ASTM standard to be changed to prohibit the use of toys of this particular shape.

Delgado v Markwort (Plaintiff):

The product involved was a **FLAG-FOOTBALL** belt; a police-woman was playing Flag Football when she got her (trigger) finger entrapped in her opponent belt's D-Ring, crushing her finger. Because of the belt's closure, I testified that this product was unsafe as designed. I testified in court at 60 Center Street, Manhattan, NY. (This building is frequently shown on *Law & Order*).

Alvarado v Bagon Marketing (Plaintiff):

The product involved was a toy **HELICOPTER**: an adult male while playing with the toy, was struck by the helicopter's roto-blades, sustaining severe injury to his eye. Because of the absence of a ring around the blades, I testified that this product was unsafe as designed.

Pooler v IKEA (Plaintiff):

The product involved was a five-drawer **DRESSER**: a 2 year old boy stepped onto the bottom drawer, and went to retrieve his diaper, when the Dresser tipped over, crushing the child. Because the Dresser was not sufficiently stable, and no attachment hardware was supplied, I testified that this product was unsafe as designed. As a result of my report, this model of IKEA Dressers were recalled.

Cirigliano v Delta (Plaintiff):

The product involved was an Infant **CRIB**: a 6 month old infant was found to have wedged himself in a gap between the mattress and the crib's disengaged drop-side rail, suffocating the child. Because the rail was not properly constructed, I testified that this product was unsafe as designed. As a result of my report, many Delta cribs were recalled; and all cribs with drop-side rails are now prohibited.

O'Sullivan v Aquarian Pools (Defense):

The product involved was an in-ground **POOL**: an adult dove off the deck into the shallow end of the subject pool, hitting the pool bottom. I testified that the pool was properly installed and met all applicable standards, and was safe.

Nedblake v Kids II (Defense):

The product involved was a child's **BOUNCER**: a 4 month old infant was properly buckled in, but was found to have her upper body slumped in the subject bouncer. I testified that the bouncer's restraint system met all applicable standards, and was considered safe.

Chapman v BestRest (Defense):

The product involved was an adult day bed **MATTRESS**: a 15 month male infant climbed onto his sister's bed, and suffocated when he got stuck between the mattress and the bed-rail. I testified that the mattress met all applicable standards, and was considered safe.

Arm's Reach v Simplicity (Patent):

The product involved was an Infant **COSLEEPER**: The subject product was being imported and appeared to violate the plaintiff's patent; I testified that the defendant's product was in violation of said patent.

Battle Toys v Lego (Patent):

The product involved was a game which featured rotating **FIGURES**: The subject product appeared to violate the plaintiff's patent; I testified that the defendant's product was in violation of said patent.

227

Infant Monitor

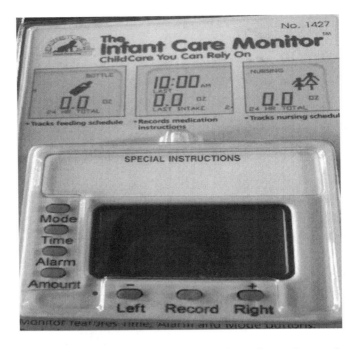

During 1995, Helaine and I developed an innovative, hand-held device to track mothers to nurse, bottle feed, diaper and medicate their infants. During the first year, at each doctor's visit, parents are often asked detailed questions about their eating schedule, and their bowel movements and medications. The unit can be set to monitor both bottle feedings and nursing schedules. We patented this idea, and on November 25, 1997 we were awarded patent #5,691,932 called the "CARE GIVER DATA COLLECTION & REMINDER SYSTEM". We sold a license of our idea to *Sanitoy,* who placed a 25K production order with REINER Associates.

When the Apple and Android phones came out, there were many APPs that had features that did the same thing, violating our patent. I contacted (149) of these companies, and for a 6% royalty fee, gave (31) companies a license to use our patent. Helaine and I split $64,000 in royalties.

My 80th

On June 10, 2017, our kids gave me the greatest present ever, an 80th birthday party, held at Helaine & Harold's home in Ridgefield. Present were family and friends from both near and far. In lieu of gifts, I had asked for contributions to either 'St. Jude' or 'Out-of-the Crate'. The following was my thank-you speech:

"I would like to thank you all for coming to celebrate my big day. One advantage of becoming 80, I won't be hounded by life insurance agents. You've come from many far lands, from as far North as Canada, South as FL; West as CA and East as ME; I really don't deserve such good friends and family.

I also want to thank my GREAT kids... Helaine & Harold, Eric & Gail, Dana & Angela for preparing (and paying) for this bash; also to Sandy my LOVING wife of 57 years, who bore these great kids! Let me start from my beginning-

80 years ago, I was born in Dresden, Germany. My father worked in my grandfather's department store Kaufhaus Reiner. As life became unbearable for Jews; shortly after Kristalnacht, my parents decided to emigrate to Shanghai.

By age 10, I had survived the war, living in the Shanghai Ghetto under Japanese domination. I attended the Shanghai Jewish School, studying English, Chinese and Hebrew, and spoke German with my parents at home.

By age 20, only a few years after my family had immigrated to the U.S., my father died (at an early age of 50), during my sophomore year at RPI. I was an only child, but by marrying Sandy, I gained a wonderful, much larger family; CARYL and the Ashkin clan who traveled from Ontario, Buffalo, Rochester, and Pennsylvania. And also the Weisberger clan who traveled from Maine, Ohio and Florida.

By age 30, Sandy and I were then living in Wallingford. It was here that we had had these great kids HELAINE, then ERIC, followed by DANA. I decided to join the toy industry, and worked as an engineer at the A. C. Gilbert Co. their motto: "there was a Gilbert toy for every boy". This is where we met our lifelong friends CAMILLE, LOUISE, SANDY & REBECCA who are here tonight; also Iris and Nate whom are represented by their daughter BARBRA.

By age 40, I had joined Coleco where I traveled Overseas extensively (at times 3-5 weeks at a time); my kids barely knew me; while Sandy, very capably took care of our home, our three kids and dogs.

By age 50, I had become Sr. VP at Coleco (remember Cabbage Patch)? That's where I worked with MARK and PAT, close friends in Las Vegas who honored me by flying cross-country.

By age 60, I had good news (the birth of our grand-children ZACHARY (now furthering his music career in Brooklyn), then ARI (now studying for his PHD at Berkeley), then JORDAN (just graduated from Emerson) and AARON (will be entering his junior year at RIT). Also the bad news; with Coleco filing chapter 11. So, that's when I started my consulting firm, REINER ASSOCIATES! We became bi-coastal and bought our 2nd home in Las Vegas; where we spend lots of time with DAVID, who drove 3000 miles cross-country, to help me celebrate here today!

By age 70, came more grand-children, SYDNEY, PJ, LUCAS and AVA, who now total eight (the Chinese regard eight as a very healthy omen). We sold our home at Lakeridge (but kept our dear friends ROY and JUDY who are also here). We bought our 2nd home at Oxford Greens, where we are surrounded by our good friends TERRI and FRANK; CHARLIE and ARLENE; GAIL and ART; CHUCK and NORMA;   CRAIG and CLAIRE all celebrating with me. I'm also hoping to reach my mother's longevity; she passed on her 102nd Birthday!

At age 80, what's in store for me next? To an Africa Safari next month, and only good things to be shared with all my GREAT friends and family! Hope to see you all for my 90th.

Thanks for coming".   *Bert*

The following list of queries were presented to this group, by my grand-daughter Sydney:

1. **Bert has been bitten by which of the following**?
a)Dog, b)Cat, c)Bird, d)Lizard, e)All of the above.

2. **Bert has had which of the following pets**?
a)dogs, b)alligator, c)cat, d)crickets, e)Japanese Beetles, f)snakes, g)rabbits, h)all of the above.

231

3. Which of the following has Bert wished he owned?
a)monkey, b)Grey African parrot, c)horse, d)ocelot.

4. Which of the following foods will Bert not eat?
a)sea cucumber, b)lungs, c)brain, d)expired foods.

5. What is Bert's preferred mode of communication?
a)memo, b)newsletter, c)text, d)eMail, e)telephone.

6. What has Bert not put into his Newsletter?
a)grandchildren's GPA, b)notification of a party to those who were not invited, c)birthdates, d)deaths.

7. Which has not been Bert's hobby?
a)bonsai, b)stamp collecting, c)tolling, d)mosaics.

8. Which of the following sports has Bert not tried?
a)boxing, b)soccer, c)golf, d)swimming, e)skydiving, f)scuba diving, g)racquetball.

10.Which sport does Bert love to watch?
a)football, b)baseball, c)basketball, d)curling.

11.What is Bert's favorite movie?
a)50 Shades of Grey, b)Pink Panther, c)Dr Zhivago.

12. Which activity did Bert not do in college?
a)sprinkled chemicals on landlord's floor, b)served dog-food to fraternity brother, c)stole garbage truck.

13. What has Bert done so right in his life?
a)great father and grandfather, b)devoted son, c)wonderful human being, d)all of the above.

My primary item on my bucket list was to travel on an African Safari. We went. The following was our daily itinerary:

Day1+2: We traveled to Zurich, Switzerland then to Nairobi, Kenya, via Business-First, Swiss Airlines; (18 hours long) but pleasant flights.

Day 3: Today we went to an elephant orphanage, we petted and fed baby elephants of three months to two years old. We also fostered a baby elephant AMBO. We then went onto a giraffe sanctuary, they do have the longest tongues! Sandy bought a hand-carved cane.

Day 4: Today's trip was HELL, we drove for 8 hours from *Nairobi* to *Serengeti* in Kenya on VERY rough roads (known as an *African massage*). It's a private tour, so it's only Sandy, me and the guide travelling. When we arrived, the 'tented' hotel *Ashnil Mara* was magnificent (see above), nicest resort we've ever been in!

Day 5: Today we left at 6:30am (because of the heat, the animals generally sleep at noon). We witnessed the *Great Migration*, what a site, we saw THOUSANDS of wildebeest and zebra in search of water and greener pastures. We also saw lots of giraffe, elephants, baboons, lions, Cape buffalo, leopards and gazelle. At night, because of wild animals roaming, we were always escorted by an armed *Maasai* whenever we wanted to leave our tent.

Day 6: Today we visited a *Maasai Mara* village. We saw the Maasai do local dances, followed by our passing out to their children crayons, coloring pencils, scissors and books. (63) kids showed up, but we only brought enough for a dozen; so some only got one crayon.

233

Day 7: Today we crossed into *Tanzania*. We travel by pop-up open-roof 4WD Land Cruiser. Saw more animals including hyenas, mongoose, cheetahs, and a pride of lions having just feasted on a zebra. The *Serena Safari* Lodge was phenomenal, very elegant, even had Wi-Fi, but hot-water for showers was limited to only 2 hours each morning. No TV (but we're too tired to watch anyway)..

Day 8: Today we left at 6:00am for an all day game drive at *Ngorongoro Crater*, the world's largest volcanic caldera (crater floor). This is a virtual Noah's ark, inhabited by almost every species of wildlife indigenous to East Africa, including over 4,000 elephants.

Day 9: Today we drive to *Lake Manyara*. It's a huge lake loaded with hundreds of species of birds, where we saw thousands of flamingos, also storks and hippos. In the afternoon, we returned to the lodge for my nap. Shortly thereafter, Sandy screamed when a baboon jumped into our room, grabbed her bag of hats (purchased that day), and a package of gum. The female baboon discarded the hats (not to eat), and passed the gum out to her family (which they all spit out- didn't like the peppermint). **What an exciting day!**

234

Day 10:On an African safari, there is no decaf, no tuna-fish, no bacon (they're Muslin), no to-go cups, no TV, few bathrooms (enroute); but we're having loads of fun! Today we saw lots of baboon families, warthogs, dik-dik, waterbuck, wild-dogs, antelope, hyenas, black-faced monkeys, and blue monkeys (yes blue). We shopped, shopped, and shopped for wooden souvenirs for all our kids and friends. At a jewelry shop I bought a set of Tanzanite earrings and matching bracelet for Sandy.

Day 11:We traveled to another reserve the *Tarangire National* park; saw more, and more animals. Saw two lionesses chasing and catching a gazelle. This evening we had a night-game drive, accompanied by a Maasai warrior (to point out the animals), and anarmed Park ranger (for our protection).

Day 12:Today was all day traveling, saw more animals, and stopped to visit our guide *Aresto's* home, to meet his wife and daughter, in *Arusha*. (Their entire home is no larger than my kitchen). Then, some more animal viewing, then onto a magnificent tree-house built on the side of a rock terrace. We could see the snow-covered Kilimanjaro in the distance.

Day 13:Today (our last day) we travelled to the *Amboseli Game Preserve*, back in Kenya, to see more animals. We've now seen all of The Big 5, except for the elusive, and protected, Black rhino. Poachers seek and kill these magnificent rhinos for sale of just the horn, for use as a medicine in some Asian countries. A total of 1,028 rhinos were killed in Africa last year.

Day 14: Our trip is over, we're at the Swiss first class lounge awaiting our flight to Zurich, while I'm writing the last of my trip itinerary. Sandy and I had both agreed that this was our best trip ever!

My Hobbies

Stamps & Coins:

I started collecting stamps after my father passed, when I inherited his U.S. collection. He got the stamp-collecting 'bug' from his friend *Irwin DeJong* who was a stamp dealer in both Shanghai and New York. He was also an artist who professionally repaired (expensive) stamps. I now collect the following mint stamp sets:

(a) Israel tabs, (complete, except for 1948).
(b) U.S. Regular and Commemoratives,
(c) U.N.-New York, Geneva, Vienna (complete to 2014)
(d) Royal wedding of Charles & Diana (on 7-29-1981)
(e) Manchuria,
(f) East Germany.

I also collect coins, particularly:
(a) annual U.S. proof sets,
(b) Washington and Liberty Quarters,
(c) State quarters (1999-2010).
(c) U.S. Type coins from ½ cent to $20 gold,
(d) Atlanta Olympic set (1996).

After I'm gone, I sincerely hope that Eric's kids will continue with my stamps, and Lucas with my coins.

R/C Planes & Boats:

237

As a teenager, and continuing into my married life, I built and flew radio-controlled model planes. I would build the plane from a kit, then add the gas-engine, servos and radio receiver; and fly them at Stratford Airport. I was an active member of the AMA (Academy of Model Aeronautics). The radio was not too accurate (I couldn't afford the better ones) so the plane would often fly off and get lost. As I had my name and phone number pasted on the fuselage; with a reward, I always got it back. My planes strayed, but retrieved from the Long Island Sound, in Bridgeport and in the woods of Peterborough, Canada.

I had built an R/C Boat which I called "MY DREAM"; for which Sandy built the furniture and accessories. It even had lights and a radio. I sailed it on neighborhood ponds.

Later on, I also built an R/C Helicopter. It was challenging to build, but very difficult to fly. Once, I got hit by the rotating blades, almost cutting off my nose.

Tropical Fish & Bonsai:

I started with a fresh-water tropical fish tank when I was a teenager, then after our marriage (when I could better afford it), had a salt-water tank which was built into the wall.

I also grew and trained *Bonsai* (miniature trees). This Japanese art-form uses cultivation techniques to produce small trees in pots that mimic the true shape and scale of full-size trees. When we lived in Wallingford, I had a garden filled with various bonsai, including Elm, Fichus, Juniper, Azalea, etc.

STORY: Both Dana and I took classes in learning how to prune and cultivate Bonsai. (One of the types of Bonsai is known as 'formal upright', in class I could not remember that description, so Dana reminded me by pointing to a bow-tie). Unfortunately, when we started to travel back/forth to Las Vegas, I had to give up this hobby.

Animation Cels:
239

Years ago I started to collect *Cels*. A Cel is short for celluloid, consists of a transparent sheet on which objects are painted for hand-drawn animation for cartoon movies. My collection of original and signed Cels include:

Raggedy Ann & Andy,	Fred Flintstone,	Donald Duck
Mickey & Minnie,	Woody Woodpecker,	Pluto
Batman & Penguin,	Monsters,	Rugrats,
Cat-in-the-Hat,	Tom & Jerry	W.C. Fields
Dennis the Menace	Laurel & Hardy	Snoopy

3D Pictures:

240

I started another hobby of creating 3D pictures, called 'Tolling' or 'Decoupage'. This is a pop-art form that was made famous by *Charles Fazzino* whose pictures sell for thousands. I would find a picture that I liked, print six copies, then cut them out into different layers, then glue them in place with clear Silicon Rubber. I was quite good at it, and even taught 3D classes while living at Lakeridge. Note the above picture of Jordan looking into a mirror.

My Genealogy

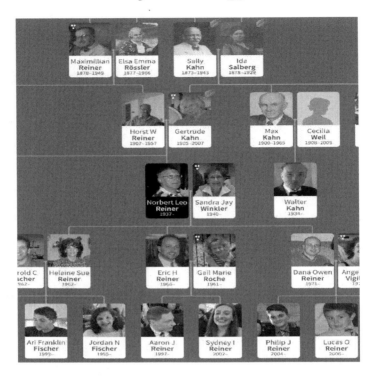

When I visited *Phyllis Weisberger* to attend *Bill's* unveiling, I noticed a software program in her computer *'Family Tree Maker'*, with a huge amount of data about our family. I was told that no one was updating this family data, so I volunteered to do so. I then subscribed to *'Ancestry'*, joined the *'Genealogy Club of Oxford Greens'*, the *'Jewish Genealogical Society of Connecticut'* and the *'Jewish Genealogy Society of Southern Nevada'*. In the REINER family tree, I now have 2,800+ family and related members.

Some years ago I did my DNA testing through Ancestry.com, and found my origin was (not surprisingly):

81% Ashkenazi Jewish
13% Germany
6% Russian

Through the DNA study, I found out that I have almost a thousand 3rd and 4th cousins, but I've been too busy to track them all.

STORY: In 2017, *Kimberly Kaminsky* a travel agent (whom I did not know), toured the Shanghai Ghetto with my friend *Dvir Bar-Gal* as her tour guide. She noticed my name on the Ghetto Remembrance Wall, and remarked that my name sounded familiar. She called her mother, who informed her that she and my mother were 1st cousins. When we later met in Las Vegas, we found out that the pawn-shop *Beauty & Essex* owned by her daughter *Jennifer* (2nd cousin once removed), was part of the restaurant owned by Sandy's cousin's son *Noah* (1st cousin once removed); is that a coincidence?

A great TV program to watch is *"Finding Your Roots"* starring Henry Louis Gates Jr., on PBS.

Feb 20, 1962 – NEIL ARMSTRONG LANDS ON THE MOON.

Nov 22, 1963 – JOHN F. KENNEDY ASSASSINATED.

Jun 6, 1967 – SIX-DAY WAR BETWEEN THE ARABS AND ISRAEL.

Sep 5, 1972 – ISRAELI ATHLETES MASSACRED AT MUNICH OLYMPICS.

Oct 6, 1973 – YOM KIPPUR WAR BETWEEN ARABS AND ISRAEL

Sep 7, 1978 – CAMP DAVID ACCORD SIGNED BY BEGIN AND SADAT.

Nov 9, 1989 – BERLIN WALL FALLEN.

Aug 30, 1997 –PRINCESS DIANA KILLED IN A PARIS CAR CHASE.

Sep 11, 2001 –TWIN WORLD TRADE TOWERS ATTACKED.

My Golf

When we sought to buy our home in Las Vegas, we decided on a house situated on the 8th hole of the *Siena Golf Club*. Although I had never played golf before, we bought it for it's location; with such a magnificent view (at a $70,000 premium). Later, I was intrigued with those guys playing with a little white ball, so I started to play. Is that Tiger Woods giving me lessons?

When in Las Vegas, I play each Tuesday with *Ira Rosenmertz*, *Walt Rogers*, *Bob Albrecht* and/or *Leo Mahasky* at the *Angel Park GC*. Our golf-club at Siena for me is too difficult, it has 84 sand-traps, some are over 6 feet deep. When in Connecticut, I play Thursdays with a mixed four-some (Oxford Greens), at the *Pomperaug GC* in Southbury, CT. Why are so many smart guys playing this stupid game?

June 28, 2010 was an unhappy day when my brother-in-law and best friend, Marvin died on the first hole of the *Pomperaug Golf Course*. After he hit his first shot, he fell down. In spite of my CPR, followed by EMT and ambulance, he never recovered. If you have to go, what better way to go!

Holocaust Survivors

Because I survived the Shanghai Ghetto; I belong to the Las Vegas *Holocaust Survivors* group, where we meet every few months. On April 4, 2013 and again on May 8, 2019 on *Yom Hashoah* (day of remembrance) the Holocaust group was invited to meet with our Governors *Brian Sandoval,* and later with *Steve Sisolak,* at the governor's mansion in Carson City, NV. Also attending was Dr. Miriam Adelson. We flew there by courtesy of *Sheldon Adelson's* (CEO of *Venetian Hotel & Casino*) private 747 jet, normally used to fly to Macao and Israel. The pilot announced this was the shortest trip he'd ever taken.

While attending a Holocaust meeting, I met *Evelyn Goldsmith* neé *Wolpert,* who also came from Shanghai, and appears with me (at age 7) in a Kadoorie school picture. I met *Gary Sternberg*, who also had come from Shanghai. I receive a small quarterly reparation from the "*Jewish Claims Against Germany*". Every year I need to submit a notarized form that I'm still alive.

Our Health

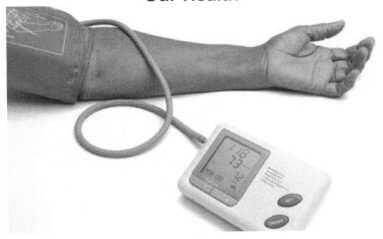

In my youth in China, I was stricken with dysentery, jaundice, typhoid fever, diphtheria, scarlet fever, hoof-and-mouth disease (for which I took gentian violet), measles and rabies (I was bitten by a rabid dog, for which I got shots in my stomach). Later on, as an adult I got Mumps (caught from Eric). When I reached my 60s, I got Type II Diabetes (for which I take insulin shots and pills).

Shortly after my brother-in-law Marvin died (June 2010), I began to complain of shortness of breath. After a routine echo-stress test, my cardiologist concluded that I was suffering from [11] *Takotsubo* (broken-heart syndrome), a temporary condition brought on by stressful situations, such as the death of a loved one. I was given a stent which corrected the problem.

In 2007 I had a deposition on a very difficult Patent case. I was deposed in a hot hotel room with five attorneys, a videographer, and court stenographer for nine hours. Afterwards, I didn't feel well and was diagnosed with *A-Fib* (irregular heart beat). Although an attempt to shock my heart *Cardio version*, it did not revert. But I've been fine since.

Sandy had been diagnosed with early *Alzheimer's* in 2016 by the doctors at the *Lou Ruvo Cleveland Brain Clinic* in Las Vegas, NV. She is now being treated by *Dr. Wint* at the *Lou Ruvo clinic* while we're in Las Vegas, and by *Dr. Cooney* at the *Adler Institute* at Yale when we're in CT. (The Lou Ruvo clinic, shaped like a collapsed building, was designed by the famous architect *Frank Gerry*). Sandy now has a hobby of 'adult coloring' (see one of hers shown above). Let me explain the symptoms of this disease:

[12]1. Memory loss that disrupts daily life:
One of the most common signs of Alzheimer's disease, especially in the early stage, is forgetting recently learned information. Others include forgetting important dates or events, asking for the same information over and over, and needing to rely on things they used to handle on their own.

2. Challenges in planning or solving problems:
Some may experience changes in their ability to develop and follow a plan or work with money. Some may have trouble following a familiar recipe or keeping track of monthly bills. They may have difficulty concentrating, and take much longer to do things than they did before.

3. Difficulty completing familiar tasks at home:
Some may have trouble driving to a familiar location, managing a budget, or remembering the rules of a favorite game.

4. Confusion with time or place:

Some may lose track of dates, seasons and the passage of time. They may have trouble understanding something if it is not happening immediately. Some may forget where they are or how they got there.

5. Trouble with visual and spatial images:

Some may have problems not remembering what they had read before, making it difficult to read a book. Some may have difficulty judging distances and determining color or contrast, causing problems driving.

6. Problems with words in speaking or writing:

Some may have trouble following or joining a conversation. They may stop in the middle of a conversation and have no idea how to continue or they may repeat themselves. They may struggle with vocabulary, have problems finding the right word or call things by the wrong name.

7. Misplacing and losing things:

Some may put things in unusual places. They may lose things and be unable to find them again. Some may accuse others of stealing.

8. Decreased or poor judgment:

Some may experience changes in judgment or decision-making. They may use poor judgment when dealing with money, they may pay less attention to grooming, and avoid being social.

9. Changes in mood and personality:

Some may become confused, suspicious, fearful or anxious. They may be easily upset at home, or when away be out of their comfort zone

Sandy became enrolled in an *Alzheimer's Drug Trial*, conducted by *Biogen*, of Boston. Unfortunately, after she had underwent 17 infusions (of the hi-dose), the trial was cancelled on March 20, 2019, as it did not help her.

Recently, I sent the following text to my kids:

"I went to a store today across town, and parked directly in front at a handicapped spot, together with Mom and our two dogs. I left the keys, in case your mother needed the a/c. When I returned, the car (with Mom) was gone, I panicked.

A lady I knew offered to drive me around to find her. We drove for nearly an hour, in and out of six parking lots, but my car could not be seen; I finally called the police. After another half hour, the police called me to say that Mom was found about two miles away, at a mall along a major six-lane road where she stopped and sought help, announcing that she was lost. As the police gave me directions; my phone battery went dead. I now had to buy a charger, then charge my phone, then call 311 to get directions, then after almost two hours, we were finally reunited! It was a very scary day."

My Religion

I was brought up in a very Jewish, but not religious, household. While living in the Shanghai Ghetto, I attended the *Ohel Moishe*, (Ashkenazi) synagogue (which is now the *Shanghai Jewish Refugee Museum*), then the *Ohel Rachel* (Sephardic) when we moved back into the French Settlement.

When we lived in Kew Garden Hills, my parents and I belonged to the *Jewish Center of Kew Garden Hills,* where I befriended *Eli Kirshblum*, our rabbi's son. We would often 'crash' Bar Mitzvah's. At RPI, I joined the *Hillel Club*.

When Sandy and I got married, we first belonged to the *Park Ave Temple* (in Bridgeport), then *Beth Israel* (in Wallingford) then *Beth El* (in Torrington), then *Beth Sholom* (in Las Vegas), then *Beth El* (in Woodbury); always Conservative. When we were first married, in consideration of my father-in-law, we kept strictly *Kosher* at home. However, we did occasionally bring Chinese and Pizza, but only into the basement or patio. When we moved to Lakeridge, we gave up being Kosher entirely.

In Hebrew, I was named *Yeshiya Ben Meir Hacohen*. Like my father (*Meir Ben Moshe Hacohen*), and my sons Eric (*Naftali Ben Yeshiya Hacohen*) and his son Aaron (*Aharon Ben Naftali Hacohen*), and Dana (*Moshe Ben Yeshiya Hacohen*), we are all KOHANIM. This means that we are descendants of Aaron (Moses' brother) the first Jewish high-priest; belonging to the tribe of Levites. Requirements of being a Cohen are that I:

(a) not come into contact or be in the same room with a deceased (except for my immediate family),
(b) be buried in the first row in the cemetery,
(c) marry a virgin,
(d) conduct *Pidyon Haben* for male first-born,
(e) be the first to get called for an *aliya,*
(f) conduct the priestly blessings on high holidays.

Sandy and I have given generously to many charities, which include monthly withdrawals to St. Jude and ASPCA. On Thanksgivings, we occasionally serve dinners at the St. Vincent Catholic Charity in Las Vegas. For years we fostered a Taiwanese girl *Wu Bei Yin*. For people's memoriam, we usually plant trees in Israel, via JNF. At our homes, we are surrounded with Judaica, i.e. Mezuzahs, Hamsas, Hanukias, Shabbat Candlesticks, signed paintings by Marc Chagall, and a picture of the Western Wall.

The following is my belief about G'd and the universe He had built:

"Let's pretend I am G'd and I set up a fish-tank: I will determine the size of the tank, select the filter, lights and heater, provide which fish to inhabit the tank. Once it's set up, I do NOT decide which fish gets sick, which fish gets eaten, which fish dies, which fish grows up healthy, etc".

My future

In conclusion, these are the wishes for my future:

Good health

Caring, loving and healthy wife

Respectful children and grand-children

Money in the bank

Sleeping in bed with our two dogs

Be in Siena overlooking the golf course & mountains

My Bucket List:
1. **Safari to Africa (*done*).**
2. **Trips through Israel (*done*).**
3. **Visit the Great Wall (*done*).**
4. **Tour the Forbidden City - Beiging (*done*).**
5. **Visit Pompeii (*done*).**
6. **Visit the Terra-Cotta soldiers – Xian.**
7. **Visit Venice - Italy.**
8. **Trip via helicopter or balloon through the Grand Canyon.**
9. **Visit the Georgia Aquarium.**

My Poem:

And then it is Winter:

"Time has a way of moving quickly, and catching you unaware of the passing years. It seems like only yesterday that I was young, just working, just married and embarking on my new life with my mate. Yet in a way, it seems like eons ago, and I wonder where all those years have gone?

I know that I have lived them well. I have glimpses of how it was back then and of all my hopes and dreams. But, here it is... the Winter of my life, and it catches me by surprise... How did I get here so fast? I remember seeing those 'older' people through the years, and that Winter seemed so far off!

But, my friends are retired and getting grey... they move slower and I see an older person in me now...But, like me, their age is beginning to show and we are now those older folks, Winter is now around the corner!

Now I enter this new season of my life, unprepared for all the aches and pains and doctor visits, and the loss of strength and ability to go and do the things that I wish I had done, but never did! Yes, I have regrets. There are things I wish I had done... also things I should not have done... Winter is so near!

My kids will soon become me... and my grandchildren will always be perfect. So, whatever you would like to accomplish in life, do it quickly. Do what you can today, as you can never be sure whether this is your Winter?

And then it is Winter"!

Bibliography:

[1] 'The Holocaust Chronicles', by Marilyn Harran, (2000).

[2] 'Shanghai Remembered', by Berl Falbaum, (2005).

[3] 'Our Family Diary', by Horace Reiner, (May 30, 1950).

[4] 'Shanghai Jewish Youth Association: It's Foundation and History', JDC file #458 (1940).

[5] 'The Fugu Plan', by Marvin Tokayer, (1979).

[6] 'Shanghai Jewish Chronicle' SMP files (Jan 12, 1942).

[7] 'Story of Bert Reiner, Toy Maker', by Kevin Ostoyich, (2017) history professor at Valparaiso University, published in the *American Institute for Contemporary German Studies*, John Hopkins University

[8] Newsweek Magazine, (November 12, 1983).

[9] 'Iacocca-Autobiography', by William Novak, (1984).

[10] 'Feng Shui', by Zaihong Shen, (2001).

[11] 'Takotsubo Cardiomyopathy', (Wikipedia)

[12] 'The 36 Hour Day', by Nancy Mace, (2018).

There are the following available videos about the Shanghai Ghetto:
"Empire Of The Sun", directed by Steven Spielberg (1987)
"Port Of Last Resort", directed by Paul Rosdy (1998)
"Shanghai Ghetto", directed by Amir Mann (2002)

Acknowledgements:

Foremost, I wish to thank my father for writing the Diary which he had presented me on my Bar Mitzvah, without which I would not have been able to write this book.

I am deeply grateful to my grandson Zachary Fischer and my friend Len Eckhaus; who both helped to edit this book. Also I wish to thank my daughter-in-law Angela for helping with the cover, and other technical IT help. And, there were so many others who have shared with me their valuable time and commented on different parts of this book. I want to thank particularly Mark Yoseloff, Len Eckhaus, and Kevin Ostoyich. None of them are responsible for any mistakes, only for their insights; I am truly in their debt.

This book is dedicated to some very people special that have been dear in my life: My wife Sandy, my children Helaine, Eric, Dana, my eight grandchildren, and my dear friends scattered around the world.

Made in the USA
San Bernardino, CA
24 July 2019